D0618347

CONNECTED

CRM™

CONNECTED

CRM™

IMPLEMENTING
A DATA-DRIVEN,
CUSTOMER-CENTRIC
BUSINESS STRATEGY

DAVID S. WILLIAMS

WILEY

Cover image: © iStockphoto.com / mikdam

Cover design: Wiley

Copyright © 2014 by Merkle, Inc. All rights reserved.

Published by John Wiley & Sons, Inc., Hoboken, New Jersey.

Published simultaneously in Canada.

No part of this publication may be reproduced, stored in a retrieval system, or transmitted in any form or by any means, electronic, mechanical, photocopying, recording, scanning, or otherwise, except as permitted under Section 107 or 108 of the 1976 United States Copyright Act, without either the prior written permission of the Publisher, or authorization through payment of the appropriate per-copy fee to the Copyright Clearance Center, 222 Rosewood Drive, Danvers, MA 01923, (978) 750-8400, fax (978) 646-8600, or on the web at www .copyright.com. Requests to the Publisher for permission should be addressed to the Permissions Department, John Wiley & Sons, Inc., 111 River Street, Hoboken, NJ 07030, (201) 748-6011, fax (201) 748-6008, or online at www.wiley.com/go/permissions.

Limit of Liability/Disclaimer of Warranty: While the publisher and author have used their best efforts in preparing this book, they make no representations or warranties with respect to the accuracy or completeness of the contents of this book and specifically disclaim any implied warranties of merchantability or fitness for a particular purpose. No warranty may be created or extended by sales representatives or written sales materials. The advice and strategies contained herein may not be suitable for your situation. You should consult with a professional where appropriate. Neither the publisher nor the author shall be liable for damages arising herefrom.

For general information about our other products and services, please contact our Customer Care Department within the United States at (800) 762-2974, outside the United States at (317) 572-3993 or fax (317) 572-4002.

Wiley publishes in a variety of print and electronic formats and by print-on-demand. Some material included with standard print versions of this book may not be included in e-books or in print-on-demand. If this book refers to media such as a CD or DVD that is not included in the version you purchased, you may download this material at http://booksupport.wiley.com. For more information about Wiley products, visit www.wiley.com.

Library of Congress Cataloging-in-Publication Data:

Williams, David, 1963-
Connected CRM: implementing a data-driven, customer-centric business strategy/David Williams.
    pages cm
  ISBN 978-1-118-83580-7 (cloth); ISBN 978-1-118-86312-1 (ebk);
  ISBN 978-1-118-86319-0 (ebk)

1. Customer relations—Management. 2. Relationship marketing. 3. Strategic planning. I. Title.
 HF5415.5.W5823 2014
 658.8'12—dc23

                                                                    2013044784

Printed in the United States of America

10 9 8 7 6 5 4 3 2 1

Contents

Preface

There is only one valid definition of business purpose:
to create a customer.

—Peter Drucker

It's been 60 years since the prolific Peter Drucker declared, "Because the purpose of business is to create a customer, the business enterprise has two—and only two—basic functions: marketing and innovation. Marketing and innovation produce results; all the rest are costs. Marketing is the distinguishing, unique function of the business."

After all this time and boundless technological progress, Drucker's fundamental truth still holds, maybe even more so today. Simply put, I believe when companies embrace an approach based on "customer strategy as a business strategy," they can create sustainable competitive advantage.

I've spent more than two decades entrenched in the customer relationship marketing (CRM) business. And although CRM has always been centered on the objective of improving relationships with customers, it has evolved from CRM 1.0, which was heavily focused on the software and technology required to manage customer relationships, to the present-day CRM 2.0, which is more about the experience. Today's focus is more about creating a direct dialog with our customers, maximizing their lifetime value, finding new customers who behave like our best ones, and ultimately maximizing return on marketing spend and shareholder value. So what qualifies me to write a book about it?

Well, I think it's safe to say that marketing executives aren't like firefighters and rock stars. Little kids don't grow up aspiring to become CRM gurus, and I'm no exception. But as it happened, I did aspire to be an entrepreneur. Instead of doodling on my notebooks in school, I was constantly sketching product designs, business plans, and organizational structures. In fact, from the time I was eight years old, I knew my purpose in life was to be a business owner. It didn't really matter what kind of business; in fact, my first proprietorship was a landscaping company that I started in college. When I was 22, I went to work as a broker for a Philadelphia-based investment bank, with the ulterior motive of finding a way to acquire a business that had a potential for greatness.

At the time, I had a client who was looking to sell his small data processing company, called Merkle Computer Systems, Inc. Having been unsuccessful at convincing him to let me represent him in the sale, I began to consider the possibility of buying it myself. With the help of an investment from another client, I began the process of acquiring Merkle in a leveraged buyout. Before I knew it, at the age of 25, I was the CEO of a $3 million company, operating in an industry about which I knew virtually nothing. As Merkle's twenty-fourth employee, I underwent the usual onboarding procedure, with sink-or-swim training on the company, industry, and business process. What had I gotten myself into?

By the early 1990s—as data collection and management methods improved and analytics became more sophisticated, working together to inform marketing programs with targeting strategies that made response rates soar—the direct and database marketing industry began to explode. I was hooked. I could see the boundless opportunity before me, and I could visualize Merkle's potential to stand the test of time. Toward that end, my unwavering objective has been to assemble a world-class team with a common commitment to building a great company and becoming a market leader. Staying at the forefront of innovation, we evolved from data processing to database marketing to customer relationship marketing, developing solutions that help the best brands in the world build competitive advantage.

Ours was one of the first marketing services companies in the industry to introduce analytics as a core service offering, attracting iconic brands such as MCI, Procter & Gamble (P&G), Marriott Vacation Club, British Telecom, GEICO, Capital One, and Dell, to name a few, who effectively launched Merkle as a brand. Many are still clients today. And with consistent 20-plus percent compound annual growth, our company has become a $350 million enterprise, placing it among the ranks of top global CRM agencies.

In my career, I have witnessed the ongoing evolution of data, analytics, and technology. As these disciplines have gained momentum in their ability to improve marketing performance, they have made an irrefutable impact on enterprise as a whole. It's true that a highly targeted, accountable, and measurable approach enables personalized customer experiences that today make true customer centricity a reality. These optimized experiences solidify relationships, encourage loyalty, and cultivate advocacy.

Consumer expectations and buying behaviors are evolving, and it's not just about the media and channels they use to interact with brands or about how tech savvy they are. It's also about a loosening of the reins with which they control their information. Today, there are generations of consumers who have grown up in the digital age. They never knew a life without the free flow of information and therefore don't feel as threatened by it. These and other dynamics are making it possible for marketers to access vast new streams of reliable customer data. Companies that use this data and master CRM as an organizational competency will thrive. To do this, brands must put the customer at the center of their business strategy. What marketers have been talking about in theory for more than a decade is now a reality. We now have the power to communicate with individual precision to the right person with the right message at the right time through the right touchpoint.

I think it's safe to say as marketers we all have an appreciation for the value a customer-centric approach brings to the success— indeed, the survival—of our businesses. In fact, I would venture to declare, to that point, that most readers of this book will say, "You had me at hello." So I've written *Connected CRM: Implementing a Data-Driven, Customer-Centric Business Strategy* to go beyond the *what* and *why*, with the intention of helping businesses delve into the *how*. How to gain vital executive sponsorship, develop overarching customer strategies, define measurement platforms, execute campaigns, and make the necessary operational preparations that will bring a customer-centric business strategy to life—in other words, how to monetize your customer strategy.

Acknowledgments

For several years now, I've wanted to write a book about the role that big data, digital, and technology play in driving customer centricity. A great deal of patience and the help of the best team in the business have proved over time what I've always known in my gut to be true: Building customer strategy as a business strategy is instrumental in fueling sustainable competitive advantage for companies. For 25 years, I have worked with colleagues whose passion for world-class customer relationship marketing (CRM) runs as deep as mine. I could realistically list a few thousand contributors who have come and gone throughout the history of Merkle's CRM evolution, influencing the philosophies that our company is built upon. And although the indirect contributors are too numerous to mention by name, a handful of individuals have lent their time, talent, and unequaled expertise specifically to the creation of this text, and to them I'd like to extend my appreciation.

To my venerable team of executive partners who work side by side with me each day, with the single-minded goal of building a great company, molding the foundation upon which Connected CRM (cCRM) is built, and guiding our team through its evolution: Thank you to Craig Dempster, Steve LaValle, John Lee, and Will Bordelon for your roles in framing this book and helping me set the vision for its message. To Jeaneen Andrews-Feldman, thank you for your tireless leadership in this effort, building the strategy for the book and seeing it through from inception to completion.

For digging deep into your experience archives to contribute the colorful stories that illustrate the power of cCRM, thank you to Brian Crockett, Ed Forman, Patrick Hounsell, Matthew Mobley, Scott Nuernberger, Marc Ruggiano, Leah Van Zelm, Peter Vandre, Kevin Walsh, Mark Weninger, and Bob Wood.

A special thanks to Sherri Aycoth, without whom this project wouldn't have left the ground. Starting with our first concept meeting and through many iterations along the way, the momentum we built gave me the confidence and discipline to make this book happen. For your countless hours of contribution, for being my sounding board, for organizing my thoughts and helping bring my vision to life, you have my gratitude.

In addition, to my esteemed colleagues within Merkle; I have had the honor of working alongside hundreds of world-class brands over the years, constantly seeking ways to optimize engagement with customers and make marketing communication more effective, more efficient, and more relevant. I would like to acknowledge these valued clients and partners, whose successes, failures, and experiences in between have been the lessons that helped shape the foundation for today's brand of data-driven, technology-led CRM. And specifically to the clients who allowed us to mention them in this book, thank you for sharing your stories that helped us illustrate the cCRM phenomenon.

And finally, thank you to my family, who patiently dodged my erratic schedule while I was juggling this book with my ongoing duties as chairman and CEO of a growing corporation. The sacrifice is not lost on me, and I am grateful for your support through my every lofty goal or impulsive whim.

One

CONNECTED CRM
(cCRM)

Chapter 1 History

There's Never Been a Better Time to Be a Marketer

Thinking back over my 25 years of leading a marketing services organization, I can't remember a better time to be a marketer. How did we get to this place of unprecedented opportunity? Today's leaders have always talked about some form of one-to-one marketing, target marketing, database marketing, direct marketing, customer-centric marketing, or customer relationship marketing (CRM). Whatever you call it, we've always known the importance of using customer data to create and manage lasting relationships. However, execution-wise, much to our chagrin, we were limited in our ability to make it real. We lacked the capabilities to utilize the massive quantity and diversity of available data in order to cultivate individual relationships across disparate customer segments, multiple channels and media, and divergent organizational silos. But now, marketers can achieve mastery over customer engagement and create lasting competitive differentiation for their organizations.

In the past quarter-century, those in the field of marketing have made tremendous progress in using analytics and information to create effective media targeting strategies and maximize media reach and efficiency. The use of data has had a meaningful impact on marketing and, in fact, led to the extension of the entire subindustry of direct marketing. From 1990 to 2010, that industry experienced immense growth, primarily as a result of the highly targetable nature of the discipline and the impact of advanced analytics, which have become the foundation of today's CRM. Historically, CRM has largely been about creating relevant messaging, effective targeting strategies, efficiency of marketing spend, and so forth. It was more about finding specific application vendors that could drive great results for more narrowly defined media and targeting objectives, such as boosting campaign response rates, improving call center efficiencies, and increasing sales conversions on the website. We became incredibly skilled at developing very sophisticated modeling techniques, which dramatically improved results. And the direct marketing industry exploded.

But the most important component of a truly customer-centric strategy remained elusive: the connections among all the working parts. We couldn't effectively bring together the comprehensive customer and prospect data from all the various media and channels—their characteristics and preferences, their expectations and demands, their purchase motivations and behaviors.

Even as access to more diverse sources of data from numerous online and offline customer touchpoints began to increase, we lacked the technology and expertise to process it in aggregate and gain insights from its bounty. The high-level models we were building were only as predictive as the data that fed them. Our analytics didn't incorporate the rich, powerful, and diverse data that today allows us to build the exceedingly complex models that drive more meaningful results. Where analytical proficiency traditionally drove results more narrowly centered around media and channels, it now encompasses the entire customer experience.

My prediction is that if we put that same analytic strength into the broader viewpoint of building customer strategy as a business strategy, we will see a similar explosive impact on industry growth. When I say "customer strategy as a business strategy," I am talking about building the entire approach to business strategy based on the needs, behaviors, and lifetime value of customers across the gamut of the relationship, from marketing and sales to service and billing. A whole new breed of business model has emerged based on this concept.

A pioneer in building a world-class brand around a customer-centric business strategy, Capital One really got it right early on. From a media-based perspective, the financial giant took an unprecedented approach to building its business around direct mail and loyalty. Starting off as a small credit card spin-off of Signet Bank in the mid-1990s, the startup has become one of the most powerful players in a market full of deep-rooted giants. Its "What's in Your Wallet?" campaign and corresponding rewards program uses an information-based strategy that revolves around the customer and incorporates analytics, technology, and a deep, vast proprietary database. As a classic channel example, think of Amazon, which built an empire by creating a world-class consumer experience and used information to create competitive advantage. The e-retailer came out of the gate with the ability to observe, analyze, and understand purchase behavior to expose customers to the most relevant content and make meaningful recommendations at every interaction. This placed it leaps and bounds ahead of less customer-centric competitors right at the outset.

At the risk of stating the obvious, it's true that data capture is at the heart of CRM. To target at an individual level, you must have some way to connect each data point to the individual. In the early years of customer-centric marketing, all we had were names and addresses of customers and prospects. Our objective was to collect as many names and addresses as possible so that we could mail printed pieces to them. Then telemarketing evolved, and the effort shifted to compiling as many phone numbers as we could possibly connect to our customers and prospects. Then along came e-mail and the endeavor to bring electronic communication to scale. You get the picture.

With the proliferation of digital channels—indeed, the explosion of available data sources—analytic engines are now sifting through cookies, IP addresses, social handles, and any number of other digital identifiers. The granular-level data enables us to gain a more complete picture of the consumer; to allow for broader, yet more targeted, communication; to gain insights that show not just how, when, and where to reach them, but also what they're doing and what motivates them to act. We have come to a tipping point, where the amount and variety of data, combined with the analytical chops to build ever more sophisticated models, are enabling insights that drive savvy marketing decisions and ensure more meaningful customer interactions. What was only theory just a few short years ago is now a reality.

In the past 5 years, my team and I began to realize the planets were aligning in such a way that, for the first time, we would be able to create true multi-channel personalization and addressability, capabilities that we knew would fundamentally change the ongoing experience of each individual customer. We became determined to understand how to monetize this opportunity for organizations. Were we finally in the sort of new world in which we could create sustainable competitive advantage?

About that same time, as the economic downturn began to have massive implications on both the marketer (in terms of budget) and the consumer (in terms of behavior), organizations started requiring more accountability from the chief marketing officer (CMO). Marketing spend was studied with more scrutiny than ever before—and that trend hasn't let up. But I tend to look at that accountability from a different perspective. The way I see it, today's CMOs have a greater opportunity to play a critical role in the growth and performance of their organizations. The boardroom has never been more responsive, more focused on achieving a common outcome of growth. Customer-centric marketing isn't merely a tactical marketing implementation plan; executed correctly, it's a fundamental shift in the enterprise framework, which in turn causes a forward shift in the organization's trajectory. It elevates the marketing discussion to the executive level of the business and becomes a key enterprise mission—and a new source of visibility and accountability.

The C-suite, the CMO in particular, is now at a critical juncture, with a real opportunity to take a strategic seat at the executive table. The CMO can take the reins of customer strategy and lead the organization in creating and driving accountable business performance through marketing. CMOs who are successful will be able to draw a straight line between marketing performance and customer behavior.

The challenge in entering this new level of visibility and accountability is that CMOs are now required to flex new muscles in broader business and finance disciplines. A prerequisite to success is understanding technology, analytics, and emerging media platforms and how they will drive performance. Financial acumen will be a new premium as CMOs validate and articulate how their work is directly affecting growth, profits, and ultimately shareholder value.

Shifts of this magnitude are rare but sweeping—and enduring. The current state of marketing can be compared with only two other major eras in the history of our line of work. Think about the brand revolution of the 1950s. The advent of national broadcast television and coast-to-coast distribution networks created iconic brands. Powerhouses such as Tide, Budweiser, and Chevrolet swept the nation, taking control of the consumer landscape. In a relatively short period, they put hundreds of small companies out of business. It was a *Mad Men* kind of world, where domination was driven by mass marketing and advertising strategies that the mom-and-pops just couldn't manage. Competitive differentiation was achieved not by quality or service but by pure reach. And the ride at the top was a long and profitable one for such mega brands.

As consumer information became more available to marketers and Internet commerce began to take shape, we entered another pivotal marketing era of direct response. The channel revolution of the 1990s and early 2000s was marked by more precise targeting and measurable outcomes, made possible by digital technology and the widespread adoption of the Internet. We watched as a new crop of e-commerce innovators such as eBay, Amazon, Netflix, and Expedia made website purchasing commonplace—and changed the meaning of "going shopping" forever. This was a major disruption, as these newcomers supplanted the tried-and-true mass retailers who couldn't move fast enough to make the shift. Giants such as Borders and Blockbuster suffered the consequences. And by the way, when was the last time you stopped by your local travel agent's office to book a family vacation?

From an organizational perspective, even the companies that were making the shift to digital were doing so with whole new divisions, erecting silos that inhibited enterprise synergies—silos that limited their ability to utilize all available customer data to its full potential and that made measurement and attribution nearly impossible, silos that would later prove arduous to dismantle and assimilate.

Throughout both the brand and channel eras, there were clear winners and losers, and the brands that gained competitive advantage were those that willingly and skillfully seized the opportunity presented by advancements in technology and shifts in consumer behaviors.

As the age of the channel progressed, the onslaught of social and other digital media steered the buying populace into uncharted territory. Today, we're in the midst of an all-out customer revolution, fueled by empowered consumers who have a plethora of offline and digital tools to help them make their own purchase decisions—and they know how to use them. The immediacy and diversity of these tools are driving consumers to take control of how and when they engage with brands, and with one another. As a result of such rapid and widespread change, according to a study of marketers conducted by Adobe, 76 percent of marketing decision makers say that marketing has changed more in the past 2 years than it has in the past 50.[1]

The data story now flows both ways. It's not just about marketers having access to heaps of consumer data. It's about understanding that consumers also have access to volumes of information about your brand, your products, your reputation, your followers, and your haters. Of course, we all know that social networks have become heavily trusted purchase advisors. In fact, according to a recent consumer study, as many as 81 percent of respondents say their purchase decisions are directly influenced by the recommendations of their networking peers, and 78 percent said their purchase decisions were affected by social media posts from the companies.[2] Customer expectations are shifting as friends, business connections, bloggers, consumer advocacy groups, and yes, the brands themselves, share ideas and experiences that influence the consumer's feelings.

Historically, the mark of distinction among companies that have successfully navigated through these massive waves of marketing change is *competitive advantage*. Survival comes down to who can find the most effective ways to deal with change and capitalize on the opportunity it creates. I think today we are in the throes of another one of those pivotal eras. My guess is that over the next 5 to 10 years, the people who master marketing in the new age of the customer will have true breakout growth and differentiation within their competitive landscape. Marketers such as MetLife, GEICO, Zappos, and Netflix stand out for me as sitting among today's top contenders in their categories.

Digital media and channels continue to evolve into unprecedented levels of customer addressability at massive scale, with the advent and proliferation of digital "audience platforms" such as Facebook, Google, and Twitter. Even retailers such as Amazon and eBay are bringing together huge audiences on digital platforms, creating opportunities for big marketers to identify and market to individuals in ways they never could before—and at every level, from name and address, to cookie, to device ID. Aspects such as behaviors and intent can be predicted and targeted. We can target an individual based not only on who he or she is at an e-mail address level but even on what that person is shopping for.

Going forward, these platforms will be the stages upon which virtually all productive consumer engagements are performed. And they are changing rapidly; it seems new ones are emerging or evolving in their capabilities every day (think of the growing scope of Pinterest or Snapchat). In order to master the platforms and their capabilities, it is critical that customer-centric marketers also master their own ability to understand and capitalize on the scale and the massive opportunity that platform marketing represents.

Take Amazon as a platform; a life insurance company can target new mothers online based on the fact that they're first-time buyers of parenting books, or a home improvement retailer can target shoppers based on the purchase of do-it-yourself idea books. The possibilities are virtually limitless, with a level of scale and precision that we only dreamed of five years ago. And over the next few years, we're going to see a whole new breed of marketer, as the role transforms from the traditional brand or direct marketer to the platform marketer. Suffice it to say this is a game changing phenomenon, and it will be the impetus that creates the next generation of marketers.

It is essential that meticulous preparations be in place to take advantage of the opportunity. That's not to say that every marketer needs to go about those preparations in the same way. Different industries lie on different planes of a digital transformation continuum (Figure 1.1).

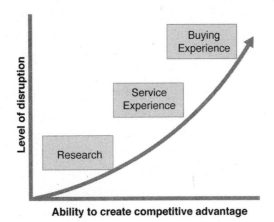

FIGURE 1.1   Digital Transformation Continuum

The continuum represents the degree to which digital is disrupting the relationship between the consumer and the marketer. The greater the disruptive force, the greater the competitive differentiation. At the most basic end of the spectrum is research. Here I'm referring to companies whose digital footprint revolves primarily around providing information for consumers who use the Internet to research a company and its products in the context of their own needs and desires. The automotive industry is a great example. I can't think of many people who would go to a dealership to buy a car without being forearmed with information such as MSRP, average price paid, warranty comparisons, competitive rankings, and even social feedback from current owners. Digital has caused a disruption in the role of the salesperson, but it hasn't fundamentally changed the service model or business model for how a car is purchased. It's still far from commonplace for consumers to buy a car online outright.

Those on the service level of the continuum have taken their digital presence to a new level but still have not made a complete business transformation. Banks come to mind. With online banking, the actual relationship between the bank and the consumer is changing. I wouldn't say consumers do a lot of research about checking accounts. They may look around a little at their options, but then they sign up for online banking and the gratification is an entirely new paperless, real-time service level with their financial institution. Today, online banking is taken for granted; banks cannot compete without a robust online service model. But still, the business model doesn't fundamentally change—the basic products of a retail bank are what they are.

On the high end of the spectrum, we would find the travel industry, which has experienced massive disruption in the relationship between the brand and the consumer. Every aspect of the research, purchase transaction, and ticket download can happen online. This new paradigm in travel planning has taken customer-centric transformation to a whole new level. It has given life to a completely new set of players that didn't exist 20 years ago, such as Priceline, Expedia, Travelocity, Orbitz, and Hotwire, which have essentially rendered the corner travel agent extinct. Not only has the general business model transformed, but new, more consumer-driven business models are popping up all the time. New sites, such as Trippy, Hipmunk, and Oyster, have launched with features that include social syncing for "checking in" during vacations and responsive design for mobile and tablet users.

In theory, most businesses strive to move along this continuum of digital transformation. The question is, in any given industry, who will be that organization that causes the disruption? Will it be a beloved, long-standing brand that makes a calculated and well-led transition to customer centricity? Or will a scrappy newcomer, with big ideas and nothing to lose, blindside the whole field? Bottom line, you can be the disruptor, or you'll surely be the disrupted—and I'd much rather be the former than the latter.

Of course, there are those industries, such as consumer packaged goods (CPG), that don't inherently lend themselves to a true one-to-one business model. But because of the digital emphasis in the age of the customer, even they are making strides toward the development of more direct relationships with their customers. For example, who would have thought such a basic CPG staple as razors would ever be a direct-to-consumer online purchase? Dollar Shave Club is taking the iconic razor-and-blade business model to a whole new level, offering autodelivery of refills for only $1.00 per month. Whether this radical model is sustainable remains to be seen, but it is evidence that even the least likely of industry sectors is recognizing the market shift toward customer centricity. And if it does take off, what impact could this have on Gillette, which has cornered the market with its premium-priced razors?

Our hypothesis is that moving away from the media/targeting mentality to a customer engagement mentality is the opportunity to create competitive advantage in today's customer-driven market.

I don't think anyone reading this book will say, "I don't really understand why customer focus is so important to my business strategy." Of course we should understand the behavior of our customers; how they interact with our brand; their preferences; needs; and desires; and their value to our brand. It's not as if anyone is going to cast doubt on these philosophies. The debate is more about the transformation and implementation.

So what's the secret to success that seems to come easy for some marketers and evade others? Building an enterprise-wide customer-centric strategy can be a very lengthy and complex undertaking, involving hundreds of decisions over a long period of time. The connection of customer centricity and business strategy is embodied in an approach my team named Connected CRM (cCRM).

This book will delve into the philosophy of cCRM, first exploring the macro trends that have driven its inception and will continue to shape its future throughout all industries. Then we will take a deep dive into an execution framework that answers the question of how, with specific strategies for enterprise implementation of the cCRM approach that will drive sustainable competitive advantage in the age of the customer.

Chapter 2 Macro-Trends

A Perfect Storm of Big Data, Digital, and Direct Consumer Engagement

I believe there is a perfect storm brewing in marketing today, as the worlds of direct-to-customer engagement, big data, and digital media collide. Customer relationship marketing falls squarely into the center of it. As the marketing landscape has evolved at breakneck speed, I've been studying the forces that have brought about today's age of the customer. Three key trends are evident, driving change in the ways brands market to customers and creating enormous opportunity for marketers: the digitization of media and channels; the proliferation of social media networks at scale; and the mobility of virtually all available media and channels. These are the disruptive forces that are creating vast opportunity for marketers to establish a position of competitive differentiation.

MACRO-TRENDS

Digitization of Media and Channels

It's clear that technology is having a material impact on how consumers and brands interact. Far and away, the most important factor affecting the way consumers are marketed to today is the digitization of media and channels—and the resulting proliferation of customer touchpoints. The digital tracks left behind by constant consumer movement among outbound digital media (brand to consumer) and inbound digital channels (consumer to brand) reveals an abundance of data that enables unprecedented analysis and targeting capabilities.

Digital progress has made it possible and practical to reach extremely high volumes of consumers in a precisely targeted manner, all at a very low cost. But because the digital footprint is so fragmented, it can be very challenging to allocate budget and therefore difficult to grow that one-to-one digital marketing effort to scale.

If I put it in the context of conventional media, within 48 hours I can fairly easily figure out how to spend $100 million on television advertising. I'd have a much more difficult time deciding how to allocate a $100 million budget in digital with individual consumer touches. It boils down to "macro-scale" versus "micro-scale." Bringing digital strategies to scale one customer at a time requires skill, patience, and above all, agility.

Micro-targeting to individuals in digital media can be significantly less expensive than broad-based strategies and is extremely effective at driving meaningful relationships with customers. Best of both worlds, right? Sure, but because it is so complex an undertaking, it can be daunting for marketers who are entrenched in the traditional; plus it's easily botched. If your competitors can do it when you can't, though, you're in trouble. You can't see their individual communications with consumers, as you can with mass media or even with online display advertising. It's difficult to respond to competitive pressure here, so it stands to reason that you would want to be on the offense with your digital strategy. Be the brand that can follow the digital exhaust and build customer loyalty. Be the market leader that keeps competitors guessing about why your share is growing at a more rapid pace.

Social Networks at Scale

It's easy to put the idea of social in a box and label it "media." But really, it's so much more. As a tool, it has gone far beyond consumers seeking input from friends and family on Facebook; it includes blogs, ratings, reviews, chat rooms, forums, and advisory boards. It can encompass any number of two-way online communications among brands and consumers. It seems to me that instead of calling social a medium, perhaps it's more appropriate to call it a peer-to-peer network. Facebook is a platform not unlike network television for advertising or the U.S. Postal Service (USPS) for direct mail. It facilitates peer-to-peer communications, only in a much more interactive, multi-directional, real-time manner. And it has made a seismic impact on consumer influences and behaviors—the magnitude of which TV and the USPS could have only dreamed.

As consumers, we have always sought counsel from friends and family as a part of the due diligence conducted when making certain purchase decisions. How am I supposed to know which plumber will do great work at a fair price? Of course, gathering that information before the advent of social media was cumbersome and time-consuming. But today, it's all right there at our fingertips, all the time. It's easy to reach everyone at once, so instead of seeking out input, the challenge for consumers has become filtering it.

The same goes for marketers. Organizations are struggling to create effective strategies for utilizing peer-to-peer networks. The flow of information from brand to consumer, from consumer to brand, and from consumer to consumer has changed so dramatically that the possibilities are endless—which is part of the problem.

A lot of people are blindly throwing money at social marketing because their organizations' leaders believe they need to be there. But being "in" social marketing doesn't merely mean having a fan page on Facebook or a few executives with a large number of Twitter followers. Ultimately, social marketing will need to have accountability associated with it, and there will need to be measurements in place for people to fully feel and understand its impact, in terms of brand loyalty and return on investment (ROI).

We have already begun to see performance measurements in the display advertising space on Facebook and open graph connections. But when we really talk about social communities, social interactions, and social media fans, solid measurements aren't yet in place for brands to really understand how much money should be spent on acquiring the next fan. I mean, how much is a fan worth to you? At the same time, social engagement, with its rich data and identifiable properties, is adding dimension to our CRM databases and enabling real customer acquisition and conversion. Ultimately, this is what we will be measuring.

Moving from crawl to walk to domination requires informed decisions and real measurements. Without them, there is no accountability for pouring today's marketing dollars into social platforms.

Consumer Mobility

Let's face it; we are living in an always-on society, full of desktop, laptop, tablet, and handheld devices that give consumers the ability to access media anytime, anywhere. And with the invention of Google Glass, it will literally be right in front of their eyes at every waking moment.

Today, I can look at items in a store, scan bar codes with my smartphone, read the reviews, evaluate alternatives, shop prices, and purchase online. This showrooming concept has threatened the brick-and-mortar retailer, but big-box titans such as Target, Walmart, and Best Buy are striking back by offering price matching against e-tailers such as Amazon.

Even transactions themselves are now a wherever/whenever proposition. And it's not just making website purchases with credit card numbers or PayPal. With tap-and-pay technology and other mobile point-of-sale payment apps, such as Square and GoPayment, mobile commerce is a snap for both consumers and businesses.

MARKETERS ARE RESPONDING

The aforementioned macro-trends and other market forces all add up to an increasingly complex marketplace as channel and media options continue to multiply. They are the disruptive forces that are creating the next age of marketing opportunity.

Savvy marketers are responding with data-driven, digitally powered customer strategies and a collective business model transformation. They are beginning to realize that forcing their products into a marketplace that doesn't need them (or isn't ready for them) is not the way to achieve competitive advantage. They are slowly but steadily beginning to adopt business strategies that place the customer at the center—not just in marketing, but across the enterprise. They are focusing their attention on big data and its ability to drive customer value for the business. They are embracing the power of digital media and channels to enhance the customer experience.

In theory, customer relationship marketing (CRM) is a fairly rational field of study, but in practice, it's a highly complex system of diverse brands, products, media, channels, and operating silos—often with competing objectives and divergent measurements of success that are in direct conflict with one another.

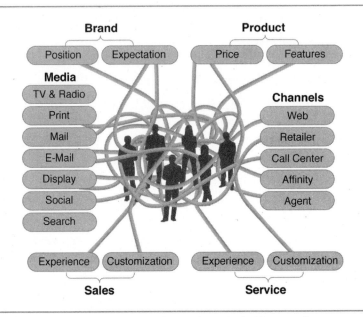

FIGURE 2.1 Complexity of Media and Channels

(Think operational efficiencies versus marketing ROI.) To be frank, it's really hard. It's really complicated. Figure 2.1 depicts the chief influencers. There are others, but these are the main factors that influence the value of a customer over time. What most people are still talking about are the things on the left: integrating digital and offline media. Media typically represents the largest portion of the marketing budget, and for most of our clients, their digital media spend is somewhere between 5 percent and 25 percent of their media budgets. If I have a $1 billion media spend, yes, that's a $250 million problem, and I have $750 million to allocate toward other activities.

Nobody talks with any great degree of confidence about complete integration of media, because very few providers can actually control everything. The discussion is not just about mass versus direct. And it's not just about managing five or six different media. It's about understanding the explosion of data from all of the disparate customer touchpoints and using it to create insights that lead to more effective, more integrated marketing decisions.

Then there is an ever-expanding channel network, representing the ways the consumer chooses to interact with the brand. There is another level of complexity associated with optimizing against omni-channel marketing strategies, which are aimed at creating consistent user experiences across customer engagement points. And on top of media and channel intricacies are the positioning of the brand, the product features, the service experience, the sales dynamic—all factors that get entangled into what really creates the experience. But with all this going on, how do I know I'm optimizing the right things? It's about making the right connections to the behaviors.

CRM EVOLUTION

It is hard to make the transition from a campaign-focused to a customer-focused mentality. This is true for all kinds of reasons. The organization itself gets in the way; campaign processes get in the way; a lack of a common language around the customer, or "currencies," makes it difficult to understand value over time; the time series necessary to make CRM work is intimidating. It's one thing to measure a single campaign at a point in time, but measuring a number of different campaigns over time—and understanding their impact on an individual customer's behavior—is quite another undertaking. As the task at hand becomes more daunting, confidence levels often begin to drop and commitment to the investment often comes into question.

Figure 2.2 depicts a functional maturity model for Connected CRM (cCRM), where level 1 represents basic direct marketing, with limited value to the overall organization, and level 5 denotes very sophisticated, *Connected* CRM, which brings a very high value to the enterprise. Most marketers, particularly in direct-to-consumer industries, have mastered levels 1 through 3. I have never been in a client presentation where everyone doesn't

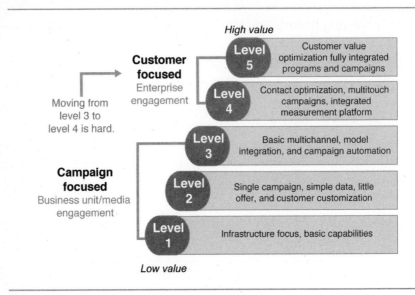

FIGURE 2.2 CRM Maturity Model

generally agree that this maturity model exists. And most of them would place themselves somewhere in the middle, banging their heads against an invisible barrier to level 4. There seems to be a glass ceiling that is preventing companies from moving past that *campaign-level* mentality that is focused on product, infrastructure, and basic modeling and segmentation. Conquering that hurdle will allow companies to cultivate a *customer-level* mentality that focuses on the experience by establishing a timed series of interactions that ultimately influence long-term customer value. But the hurdle is very difficult to clear, and the integration that paves the way for it is what cCRM is all about.

Most of the effort in levels 1 to 3 is about efficiency and effectiveness of marketing spend by tactic. Levels 4 and 5 start to focus efforts on the omni-channel customer experience, with an eye toward competitive advantage.

The concept of cCRM and its implementation framework were developed from this one phenomenon. Why are people getting stuck between levels 3 and 4? How can marketing organizations, brands, even entire industries become more customer centric?

In practice, we may end up spending a lot of money to influence consumer behaviors that show no direct monetary results in a single campaign, but their value over time will increase. Most companies have a hard time justifying that spend.

As we study this dynamic, I think there are two worlds that we ultimately need to conquer. Marketing functions are both brand and customer focused. As depicted in Figure 2.3, integration is the key to successful CRM.

First is the brand creation world. I think GEICO is really good at this. "Fifteen minutes will save you 15 percent or more on car insurance." GEICO and its advertising agency, The Martin Agency, hit it out of the brand-building park with this slogan and its surrounding identity campaign, boosting awareness that gave the company an opportunity to earn increased consideration.

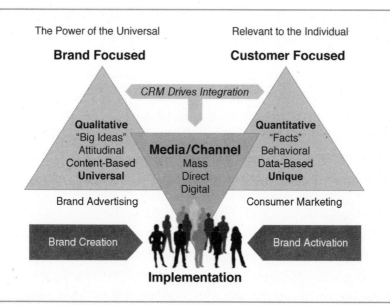

FIGURE 2.3   Integration of Brand and Customer Focus

But contrasting the brand story with the customer story, if I told a traditional brand agency that David Williams bought a Harley and has a son who is turning 16, what would they do with that? Start running nationwide commercials for motorcycle insurance? For new driver coverage? Someone needs to be able to rationalize that level of information and ultimately execute a strategy through carefully selected media—what I typically call brand activation.

The point is that there needs to be a granular level of conversation on the customer side. This is not to minimize brand at all, because I think brand is incredibly important. But the detailed customer conversation ultimately activates that brand. We need to respect the brand and understand its influence, but in the end, we make money only through the behaviors of customers. The integration really needs to live at the most granular level, and it's the customer enterprise that really holds responsibility for broad-level integration. For effective CRM, we need to connect those two ends of the spectrum and build brand with a customer focus. So that we are reaching each customer in an appropriate way, but with that universal brand identity.

As the remaining chapters of this book unfold, we will discuss the framework of capabilities and operating skills that bring cCRM to life. Before we go into that level of detail, let's distinguish between *having* a capability and *operating* it, as illustrated in Figure 2.4. If you want to create value and differentiation for your company, you have to move up through the ranks, from the most basic marketing functions to the most sophisticated enterprise-wide cCRM business strategy. To ascend through the levels, you must advance your capabilities. And even if you have the ability to integrate data across touchpoints, apply the analytics, and execute omni-channel communication strategies, who's going to run it all in a manner that incorporates customer value throughout? And by contrast, you can have the leadership mandate and organizational buy-in, but without the capability to manage all the levers, the organization

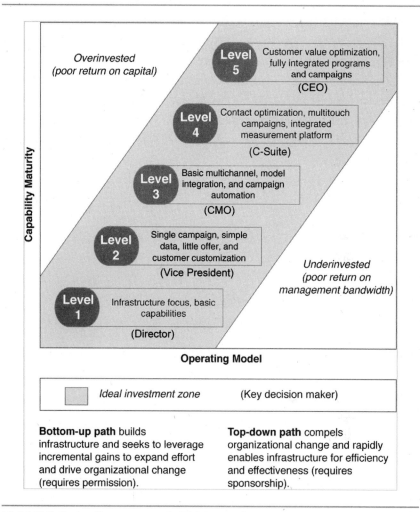

FIGURE 2.4 Connected CRM Implementation

will be spinning its wheels. So the ideal goal for bringing real value is to find the balance along the way up the continuum and try to keep the capabilities and operating skills aligned with your level of cCRM maturity.

In my opinion, the marketing services world puts too much focus on capability development. The marketplace has hundreds of suppliers who try to feed state-of-the-art point solutions to marketers. They do lots of cool things, but in a customer-centric world, that's not enough. Until about five years ago, we never saw the venture capital funding community hit the marketing space. Billions of dollars are now being funded against the technologies that are bombarding marketers with capabilities. In the end, none of those capabilities will be meaningful if they can't be operationalized.

Chapter 3 Industry Perspective
Business Model Matters

The magnified emphasis on customers, coupled with ongoing advancements in technology and the digitization of media, have enabled the evolution of traditional distribution paradigms. This new reality is creating pressure on firms with traditional business models to become more customer engaged, when in the past they were focused primarily on the intermediary. These companies are evolving in favor of direct-to-consumer business models, enhancing the customer experience and fostering durable relationships.

At the same time, companies that have been historically organized around product or channel and media are breaking down silos and rebalancing the decisioning process to begin building customer strategy as a business strategy. Enterprise needs, behaviors, and values must be considered. How much information does the company have about its customers? The customer base of a consumer packaged goods (CPG) company may contain more unidentified consumers, whereas a bank will boast a customer base full of identified consumers along with

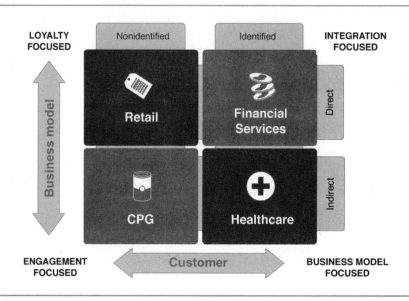

FIGURE 3.1   Business Model Matters

other robust information. This has a bearing on messaging, media, and channel decisions.

Consider the business model diagram in Figure 3.1. The horizontal axis is a continuum that represents the degree to which an organization's customers are identified, with the leftmost position being anonymous with sketchy, if any, additional data and the rightmost position being fully identified, complete with rich information. Do your customers have to identify themselves to you in order to complete a transaction? As a consumer, to get a credit card or open a checking account, I must provide detailed information about myself. But I can walk into Urban Outfitters and buy a size large blue shirt with cash without telling the staff anything. On the *y*-axis is the distinction between a direct and an indirect customer relationship. I do business directly with Capital One, but if I'm being insured by Aetna, I'm often going through my employer or an agent.

Even if the brand doesn't *sell* direct, establishing relationships with end consumers is proven to build loyalty, advocacy, and great value. Generally speaking, the way businesses in these four quadrants are attacking customer centricity—using information to better inform decisions and influence customer behavior—is radically different.

- *Integration-focused customer relationship marketing (CRM):* Companies in the upper right quadrant are the most mature today in terms of CRM. A bank, for example, can implement Connected CRM (cCRM) with relative ease. Direct, identified customer relationships, combined with detailed information shared during the sales process, gives marketers the information and access they need to execute effective CRM strategies. However, although it's true they have the largest quantity of information, in many ways that information can bog them down. At this point in their customer centricity journey, they tend to be more focused on operationalizing that information than on using it to enhance the customer experience.

- *Loyalty-focused CRM:* The upper left quadrant includes retail as an example. Customers buy directly from retailers but do not always share personal information, making it difficult for marketers to customize approaches based on customer behavior. These companies are very dependent on loyalty programs, because they need to place tremendous emphasis on the identification of customers. It's like the airlines 25 years ago. Most people don't realize airlines didn't create loyalty programs to improve loyalty per se; they created the programs to get consumers to identify themselves, because the travel agents wouldn't share detailed customer information with the airlines. Retailers are in the same position today. Cash transactions don't leave an information trail, and credit card companies can't share the information unless there is an affiliation. Loyalty programs and branded credit cards help bridge that gap, but the information may still be sketchy—and customers not involved in the loyalty program can still be difficult to know.

- *Business model transformation-focused CRM:* In the lower right corner, companies such as pharmaceutical manufacturers are very much in the throes of a business model transformation.

The nature of prescription drugs is such that these companies can't transact directly with consumers, but the access to customer information is there—and those customers are making many more of their own healthcare choices. So, in addition to the traditional emphasis on nurturing relationships with the healthcare providers themselves, pharma companies are developing strategies to build direct relationships with end consumers. They use tactics such as providing patients with in-depth information on the benefits and risks of their products, offering discounts on trial prescriptions, and developing tools to ensure patient compliance and persistence.

- *Engagement-focused CRM:* The bottom left quadrant is the toughest place to be in a world where customer centricity is king. CPG manufacturers have virtually no inherent visibility to their consumers, no easy means of gaining transactional data, and consequently, no intrinsic knowledge about them. With the retail distribution model, too many intermediaries stand in the way of that. Brands rely heavily on nonfinancial metrics, such as social media activity, to influence brand awareness and loyalty. So, as they pursue their CRM transformation, companies such as Nike are becoming very focused on engagement, using it as a proxy for transactions. They are creating campaigns with the sole purpose of engaging consumers—to like them on Facebook, join a fitness group, sign up for a sponsored charity run, or take any other action that creates a direct connection. Imagine if an agency were to pitch a campaign to a financial services company that is meant to do nothing but entice engagement—and watch how fast that agency gets fired. Financial institutions expect campaigns that yield financial results. The marketing motivations are very different between the two types of companies.

There are numerous "best practices" for companies within each of these quadrants. Brands generally have a pretty narrow lens today, and their business model itself is the key driver of the way they view their marketplace.

Progress toward customer centricity is happening at varying paces in different industries. Some are deep-rooted in a third-party distribution model without direct customer relationships, such as CPG companies. Others, such as retail banks, have achieved dominance by moving toward an integrated, customer-centric business model. As is the case in so many areas of business strategy, the key drivers of a collective industry's movement within the business model study are the companies that disrupt the status quo.

We tend to talk about business model disruptors in terms of readiness. In other words, one industry is in a better position to implement customer-centric strategies because of its ability to collect data and interact directly with customers, whereas another industry has a tougher row to hoe because of the indirect nature of its purchase paradigms. But what if we begin tying these disruptors to another dimension, such as how they actually effect changes in an entire industry's value proposition?

Revisiting the business model quadrant, think of Procter & Gamble (P&G). As a time-honored CPG brand, it sits in the lower left-hand quadrant, with a primarily indirect business model and few opportunities for direct interaction with consumers. But as a leader with eyes on disrupting the status quo in the CPG space, the company is trying its hand at disintermediation—at least partially. Of course, P&G will always want to remain relevant to retailers, but its marketing leaders are judiciously beginning to open new avenues for direct customer relationships, taking to social media and even opening a direct buying platform for consumers, much like what Apple has done so skillfully with the Apple Store. And others are following suit. In fact, according to the CMO Survey, the number of companies that intend to increase their level of disintermediation more than doubled between 2009 and 2011, growing from 15.2 percent to more than 32 percent.[1]

I believe that virtually every company is in some stage of trying to move from the bottom left toward the upper right quadrant.

The closer you are to the consumer, the more involved you can be in the conversation and the more influence you will have over perceptions and behaviors. That's why tools such as the Kraft Foods Recipes and Tips Facebook page or the Home Depot do-it-yourself app exist. But the progression between quadrants is slow. Take the CPG industry: It is still heavily focused on brand, and although some brands are dipping their toes in the direct-to-consumer model, there is not a clear breakout brand that is running away with the race. New entries will continue to jump in and shake things up. Consider, for example, Dollar Shave Club, whose platform rests entirely on the premise of social media. Who knows how successful this particular company will be? But the viral nature of its market entry has certainly caused a stir—and marketers are taking notice.

The healthcare insurance sector is traditionally a solid member of team lower right. But Patient Protection and Affordable Care Act (PPACA) means payer-customer relationships are going to become increasingly direct and move steadily along the digital transformation continuum (see Chapter 1). Kaiser Permanente is advertising heavily today with a service experience message. Health insurance consumers, who are accustomed to using digital primarily for research purposes, can now use the company's open API health app to keep track of all of their health-related matters. Whether it's medical records, doctor appointments, fitness and nutrition regimens, or payment history, customers have anytime, anywhere access to the tool. The idea is to become entrenched with the customer. So, although the decision to use Kaiser Permanente today may have been made indirectly by consumers' employers, the time will come when the choice is in their own hands. Theoretically, consumers will not want to break the well-established bond.

Auto insurance is on the fast track from lower right to upper right. Ten years ago, there was really no online relationship opportunity between companies and customers. Today, consumers can research coverage, obtain quotes, purchase, and now even file claims online, anytime, anywhere, from any digital device, including mobile. Companies such as Progressive and GEICO have taught the U.S. population to shop for auto insurance, and they've built strong relationships in the process.

Even if the direct versus indirect business model is unlikely to change, there is still great value in cultivating direct relationships with customers. Everyone is interested in the opportunity this creates. Think of a book publisher like HarperCollins. The book-buying paradigm is not going to shift such that consumers will buy their books directly from the publisher on a large scale. However, if the publisher is providing readers with content they are interested in, such as virtual reading groups, chats, newsletters, excerpts, and author profiles—plus links to online book retailers—that consumer will likely continue to revisit Harper-Collins for reading ideas.

These companies with indirect customer relationships have time to create a 360-degree view of the customers at scale and take systematic steps toward establishing enterprise-wide customer centricity. Other industries, such as financial services, which have highly identified customer bases and solid direct-to-consumer business models, are in the throes of the transformation from being product focused to customer focused. These industries don't have the luxury of time to execute on customer strategy as a business strategy. To be competitive, the time is now to begin monetizing the investments they have been making in a CRM infrastructure.

In the context of the CRM business model discussion, it is common for any given company to operate within multiple CRM business models. But as a rule, industries tend to fall into one quadrant, or sometimes hover between two quadrants. CRM approaches, by necessity, vary widely. From the operational-focused bank, to the business-model-focused healthcare payer, to the loyalty-focused retailer, to the engagement-focused consumer goods company, old habits die hard. But all businesses can profit from a customized strategy based on a business model, and many have decided to do the hard work of adopting a cCRM strategy, which pays big dividends in a relatively short period of time.

Hard work requires change—in most cases, major change. Companies organized in product, service, or technology silos will need to reprioritize around customers. Those that fail to share data among disparate functional areas, and often with business partners, will find themselves with valuable databases that are ineffective. The cCRM approach allows brands to integrate their intelligence from customer interactions and leverage it to achieve sustainable competitive advantage.

DATA AND ATTRIBUTION CONSIDERATIONS

Across the board, the role of the customer is changing. The digital media explosion has empowered consumers to take a more active role in their own purchase decisions. Their expectations have evolved, requiring brands to offer seamless interactions across all touchpoints in order to engage consumers with meaningful experiences.

The ability to acquire extraordinary amounts of data through the increased digitization of media and channels brings with it the need to harness the power of that data. Like products and services in most industries, it takes sophisticated analytics to bring a fractured marketing landscape into focus. Outbound marketing and inbound service touchpoints need to be captured, sorted, and analyzed. The marketer needs to be able to integrate the customer experience across the life cycle. This capability depends on having a connected data management platform, predictive analytics, and business intelligence.

For example, customer-centric or one-to-one marketing in the insurance and wealth management industry can be achieved only by synthesizing information across channels in a database that connects data to individuals, regardless of source. cCRM requires knowledge of the consumer as well as the capability to manage marketing efficiencies across channels. For example, in this way, a company can implement real-time bidding (RTB) approaches for buying media that go far beyond the anonymous cookie-based approach common today. Instead, they will have a true CRM perspective and an ability to estimate the long-term value of the customer.

Market leaders are building and enhancing rigorous data collection and management capabilities:

- Customer recognition: the ability to better identify customers across computer, tablet, and smartphone devices
- Omni-channel data recognition: the integration of all offline and online touchpoints into a single customer stream supplemented by first-, second-, and third-party sources
- Multi-channel marketing attribution: the capability to give fractional credit to all customer touchpoints (online and offline)

These capabilities enable organizations to examine relationships now visible through data capture and preference tracking, then true customer experience moments and discussions can be created. Data can be leveraged to learn more about their customers, and timed communications can then be developed to promote repeat purchases, planned events for the next visit, and so on. Creating the various tools to capture customer information and use it for this purpose has been the primary hurdle for organizations.

Organizations with the determination to meet the challenges of managing data in a complex marketplace will improve customer segmentation, develop personalized and integrated contact strategies, and integrate customer management—all in the pursuit of a cCRM strategy. These topics are explored in depth in Chapters 7 and 8.

INDUSTRY MATTERS

Every industry feels the impact of changing landscapes. Their business models are transforming to take advantage of new opportunities, but that transformation is being shaped by industry-specific challenges. Industry leaders can gain competitive advantage, but being out in front of the pack exploring new territory offers great risk in addition to that great opportunity. Success requires both deep marketing expertise and deep industry expertise and a cCRM approach.

The following pages explore cCRM perspectives from six major industry groupings—namely, banking, insurance, life sciences, retail, CPG, travel and nonprofit offering insights into the unique nuances of each market and ideas for approaching cCRM strategies in your own business.

BANKING

The State of CRM

After two decades of relatively small and predictable changes, we have begun to see considerable transformation in the retail banking business model. Until recently, retail banks relied primarily on three core approaches to revenue generation: traditional money exchanges (personal or business accounts), fees for services (such as overdraft), and interchange revenue from credit card transactions (earning 1 to 3 percent per transaction).

Banks that have traditionally, and comfortably, been product centric are discovering the need to become customer centric, not only in their marketing efforts, but also in the way they organize themselves and develop products. Three external factors are driving this shift. First is the regulatory environment. The Dodd-Frank Wall Street Reform and Consumer Protection Act and the Durbin Amendment led to regulations that materially impacted various fee revenue sources for banks, without allowing for corresponding cost reductions. The result has been a direct hit to the bottom line. Adding to the challenge has been the burden of an additional layer of administrative responsibility created by the Consumer Finance Protection Bureau, which has been charged with oversight of consumer financial products.

Second is the lingering financial recession, which has been slow to recover, affecting the ability to spread revenue between deposits and loans. This has placed top-down pressure on retail banks to produce profits.

And the third factor is about the way consumers research, purchase, and use financial services products in a digital world. In 2011, for the first time, more consumers opened a financial services account online than in a branch. In fact, the number of consumers who opened checking accounts online more than doubled during that time.[2] But the trend isn't limited to checking accounts; online accounts are on the rise across product lines. This is presenting both challenges and opportunities as banks learn how to attract and consultatively sell their products to clients online while still leveraging their valuable branch sales and service assets.

Industry Leaders Are Responding

Until now, banks have relied so heavily on fees and subsidized profits that they have been slow to develop customer-centric business strategies. They weren't compelled to. With the financial services industry now facing rapid change, they are responding with renewed focus on creating products and services that meet the needs of their customers, as well as on maximizing value from different segments. National and regional banks have already begun developing their customer development and integration as a means of competitive differentiation. This is a vast departure from the product and channel silo structures that dominated the industry for so long.

Retail banks are in an ideal position to make cCRM happen. Revisiting the business model diagram (Figure 3.1), they are already in the top right quadrant, enjoying the benefits of direct, identified relationships with customers. In fact, nearly every interaction is identified. This wealth of contact and interaction has provided deep demographic and behavioral information, allowing banks to understand and anticipate customer needs and thereby provide relevant solutions. However, the barriers of organizational structure and operating model are enormous in most banks, and despite the stated objectives, progress down this path has been slow for almost all banks.

The truth is, many large banks' marketing efforts currently lie somewhere between product centric and customer centric. The knowledge, resources, and technology needed for CRM require significant change, particularly in the way banks are organized. This includes emphasis on capabilities for inbound and outbound engagement and the consolidation of the customer view among all offline and online touchpoints.

The result is a united marketing group, or at least well-coordinated teams, spanning traditional direct marketing, digital marketing, and channel interaction. Together, these teams develop highly engaging cCRM programs across the enterprise. An integrated campaign approach also provides increased customer knowledge and insights, allowing for a greater focus on improving product promotions so they are more relevant and create incremental lift.

As the financial services industry moves into more sophisticated CRM and analytics, they can conduct tests and experiment with new offers, products, media, and populations with the knowledge of who their customers are and what those customers want. In the past few years, financial services companies have moved their customer communications to more digital media.

On the Horizon

For most banks, the future state of a customer-centric business strategy is diametrically opposed to their current organizational and operating models. We see banks taking many different paths in the right direction. Variations are based on individual strengths or constraints in executive vision and sponsorship, current enabling technology and capability models, and their organizational discipline around defining clear transformation objectives and leaning in against them. Most important is that investments in capabilities are planned and coordinated, encompassing the shifts in operating model and business processes that are required to apply those capabilities.

INSURANCE AND WEALTH MANAGEMENT

The State of CRM

The insurance industry's core products are life, property and casualty (P&C), and health insurance, while the wealth management industry is focused on retirement services and individual investing. Companies within these industries are experiencing a shift in the nature of competition, driving them to market more directly and personally to current and potential customers. Unlike other industries where new entrants routinely shake things up, in insurance and wealth management, the competitive dynamic is driven by changing consumer behavior, technology-fueled commoditization, and regulation.

Insurance and wealth management companies are adjusting to consumers who are increasingly digitized. For example, the way consumers research and buy products and services using digital media and devices requires marketing and technology investments that are difficult for agents and brokers to make. The insurance and wealth management companies are now making these investments themselves and finding that they can use them to create long-term, profitable direct-to-consumer relationships.

As they do, these companies are coming to understand that consumers expect an engaging omni-channel experience and seek both information and dialog online. Yet, despite this emerging understanding, few companies are fully prepared to take advantage of the available opportunities to drive competitive advantage through *experience*.

Life and P&C organizations are also adjusting to major demographic shifts in their traditional agent channels. They are learning how to develop one-to-one marketing capabilities that in some cases are opening up new distribution channels and in others are enhancing existing intermediary channels. Across the industry, they share the challenge to adjust their business model to be more centered on the end consumer.

Additionally, for auto and life insurers, the pivot toward a more customer-centric model is being influenced by price comparison–driven commoditization and an intermediary focus on a narrow set of products and services. Given these dynamics, it has become more and more difficult to differentiate, raise share of voice, or grow through traditional intermediaries. This in turn is forcing more and more carriers into direct relationships with the end customer at the point of acquisition, building on a process that began with insurers taking over policy and claim interactions from agents.

Lastly, the Patient Protection and Affordable Care Act (PPACA) created a need for healthcare insurers to deliver product and price information directly to consumers. This is a major business model shift for payers whose market and operational strategies hold agents, brokers, and products at their core.

Industry Leaders Are Responding

Insurance and wealth management marketers who understand the value of cCRM are moving closer to the customer while optimizing intermediary channels. Companies such as GEICO have led the way in direct-to-consumer marketing of auto policies and the utilization of the Web, direct mail, and sales and marketing distribution channels. These companies invested in the infrastructure, data, people, and analytic capabilities to identify, recognize, and target consumers to deliver a personalized customer experience that ushered in tremendous growth as they stole market share from traditional agent-based insurers. With the use of cCRM, the disciplines of data management, analytics, measurement, and execution can be integrated across all media and channels and optimized at the consumer level. This is a fundamental shift from yesterday's product- and media-focused process that left wide gaps between consumer insight, planning, and execution.

On the Horizon

In the next few years, the battle for competitive advantage will be won or lost by the ability to create a customer-centric, analytics-driven, real-time value chain with a strong emphasis on the digital platform. The marketing winners will identify and master opportunities to connect multiple online and offline data sources in an integrated analytic environment and execution platform across all channels in a personalized fashion tied to the customer experience. This platform will allow faster, even real-time, optimization of marketing spend.

LIFE SCIENCES

The State of CRM

The changing industry dynamics in the past five years have had a major impact on the way life sciences companies, those who manufacture and market prescription drugs, devices, and over-the-counter medicines, approach their customers: both healthcare providers (HCPs; for example, physicians) and consumers (for example, patients). Three major disruptors—reduction in sales rep access, the digitization of media, and changes in health-care policy—have drastically changed how both patients and HCPs make healthcare decisions.

Firstly, sales rep access has declined significantly. Studies show that 47 percent of primary care physicians have implemented some level of restriction on how much time they will spend with pharmaceutical sales reps, traditionally the lead driver of sales for the industry.[3]

Secondly, the number of sources for medical information (and ease of access to them) has significantly increased. This is further compounded by the fact that HCPs and consumers alike are skeptical of industry-produced information for all but a very limited set of content (for example, product support). Consumers and HCPs can now readily access more medical information than ever before, produced by sources other than life sciences companies: peers, third-party sources, and other less-reliable sources. In fact, industry-developed disease and drug website sources are only accessed between 9 and 12 percent of the time by consumers seeking treatment information.[4]

The third disruptor, changes in healthcare policy, has changed the locus of control for ultimate treatment choices, where managed care determines a significant portion of individual therapy decisions. As patients are increasingly required to have health insurance, the managed market policies—driven by the need to drive down healthcare costs—will further dominate treatment protocols.

Industry Leaders Are Responding

Taken together, these disruptions require that life sciences marketers take both a broad and deep look at their customer base, their information needs, and digital "body language" to understand how to best engage and drive effective, quality health decisions. It represents a shift in the life sciences business and sales model, now placing the end customer at the center of their efforts. For example, the traditional direct sales force model, one where brand reps travel from office to office to inform, promote, and create demand, is no longer a productive way to engage or even fully understand physicians and HCPs. By 2012, nearly one in four direct sales force interactions had been replaced by digital interactions.[5] With the significant amount of data available across traditional and digital channels, life sciences companies have an opportunity to engage, predict, and fully understand customer needs. For the industry, the next five years will shape a new way of engaging customers across all channels to deliver optimal support for healthcare decisions.

Life sciences companies recognize the need to change their approach to customer data management as they seek to move from traditional nondigital, labor-intensive data analysis to a more dynamic, automated analysis. Automation will help marketers embrace the speed and flexibility of digital interactions while also supporting personalized communications, dynamically based on how, where, and when HCPs and patients engaged. The foundation for automations is the data management capability that can accurately explain how and why customers behave. This includes capturing the data available from digital channels, developing statistical models to leverage digital and offline data, and building longitudinal customer analytics models. In this way, a pharmaceutical company can create a 360-degree view of individual customers that underpins effective customer-centric communications.

On the Horizon

A key challenge for life sciences in building next-generation marketing is lack of prior experience in this area: the process, the metrics, and dealing with the organizational barriers that impede it. Digital promotion, digital data, and analytics based on digital and offline data are all relatively new in this industry. Developing models to measure, understand, and optimize customers on a longitudinal (not cross-sectional) basis is also new. Taking action based on a unified CRM platform across all channels and advanced analytics will require changes in how promotions are developed, who "owns" the customer, and how budgets are allocated.

Tremendous opportunity exists to strengthen customer relationships—efficiently and effectively—through a customer-centric approach to integrated communications. For example, patient adherence initiatives specifically leveraging mobile service and its rapid adoption by consumers can create direct ongoing relationships with patients throughout the life cycle of treatment or diagnosis. Programs like this demand that companies have the ability to understand patient needs, track individual patient progress and behaviors, and serve them optimally with helpful resources. Complementing sales reps with representative-triggered communications to valued physicians can ensure that the next sales call is productive and the HCP receives just what he or she needs. Pharmaceutical companies can use analytics to match reps with providers based upon attitudes, indicating when to call upon a provider based on behaviors such as their recent Web searches.

These types of capabilities will mean big changes in brand plan development, interactions with suppliers, and interactions with the sales force, as well as in building links between patient and HCP promotions. Life sciences companies that embrace this path can expect highly measureable and impactful programming that ensures a focus on the most valued customers, builds relationships with growing customers, and supports patients in accessing effective treatments for health outcomes. Ultimately, deep knowledge of customers may be the companies' only significant edge in this highly competitive life sciences industry.

RETAIL

The State of CRM

Retailers are part of a vast, complex ecosystem of players known as the supply chain, which consists of CPG companies, manufacturers, distributors, wholesalers, brokers, and ultimately, consumers. These industries are driven by three dynamics—omni-channel as the new norm, device proliferation, and increasing need for greater personalization.

Within the supply chain, retailers have a direct relationship with consumers, and goods and services are provided through complex, interrelated, and rapidly evolving purchase channels. Although channels include brick-and-mortar stores, mail order (catalogs), call centers, affiliates, and rapidly growing e-commerce and mobile, the challenge lies in a retailer's ability to be nimble and engage with consumers across all of the channels, commonly referred to as omni-channel. In addition, the rise of online channels and pure-play leading e-commerce brands, such as Amazon and Zappos, combined with the digitally empowered customer, has transformed the retail industry significantly over the past 10 years.

In this digital age, consumers can shop from any device at any time of day, and price-sensitive consumers can research goods and comparison shop before making a purchase online or in a store. The availability of the same or very similar products from multiple retailers homogenizes the market. Consumers also expect a consistent shopping experience between offline and online storefronts, with the ability to find or return goods across either channel. As a result, retailers must constantly evolve to reach customers, create differentiated experiences, and compete in a highly competitive industry.

The good news is the retailing model allows for a direct relationship with consumers, and therefore, retailers, unlike CPG or pharmaceutical companies, are present at the moment of truth when a customer makes a buying decision: the point of sale (POS). From this buying interaction another opportunity arises: tailored experiences. Many small local retailers have long realized this advantage. For example, a dry cleaner recognizes a customer and has the order waiting before the customer reaches the counter. Can a much larger retailer reach this level of personalization, create customer loyalty, and drive repeat purchase? Can it do so at scale? How can personalization be extended to digital channels and media? Tailoring the experience is the new battleground.

However, there are challenges at the POS data capture and customer recognition. Most retailers do not have the means to identify all their customers at POS or during the shopping experience in order to build a one-on-one relationship. Even after investing in loyalty and rewards programs, traditional retailers are able to designate only a portion of sales to a limited universe of enrolled customers. It's both easier and equally difficult with online retail. On one hand, an online purchase requires a shipping address and creates customer identification. On the other hand, customers still browse anonymously using multiple devices before purchase.

Industry Leaders Are Responding

In response to the changing dynamics of the retail ecosystem and consumer expectations, retailers recognize the importance of putting the customer at the center of their organization across all channels. Those who have made customer strategy central to the overall business strategy are reaping the financial benefits. They have the capabilities to create sustainable competitive advantage:

- The ability to create and manage a 360-degree view of the customer through a CRM foundation

- The ability to micro-target and personalize the media and channel experience of their customers
- The ability to use customer insights to inform product allocation, promotions, and pricing strategies
- The ability to measure media and the consumer's path to purchase to improve marketing investment

By having a 360-degree view of customers, a retailer can segment and prioritize customers in terms of value and potential. For example, with a comprehensive CRM database built on POS, loyalty, or private-label credit card programs and promotional and channel data (online and offline), retailers can collect a wealth of knowledge about the purchase behavior of shoppers and better identify customers throughout the purchase life cycle. The key ingredient to success is that the cCRM model is integrated across the business into a single source, which requires organizational silos to be broken down or, at a minimum, requires them to collaborate for a shared view.

In addition, a customer-centric retail organization can best leverage insight about their customers to drive product allocation decisions, promotions, pricing, assortment, and, ultimately, inventory decisions, especially important for seasonality planning. Leading retailers have an integrated customer strategy and product strategy that optimizes the generation of demand (marketing) and the fulfillment of that demand (fulfillment, distribution, logistics, and replenishment) to best serve customers and drive growth.

In practice, this is what customer centricity looks like to an Amazon customer: What the customer sees, hears, and experiences on every visit is meant for that customer alone. Amazon seems to know more about its customers than the customers do themselves. What the customer has browsed, placed in a basket, and ultimately purchased has a huge influence on the e-mails sent to the customer, what is recommended at the site, and the overall shopping experience. Although online pure-plays have a leg up in personalization thanks to technology, traditional retailers are striving to do the same across all touchpoints and their storefronts.

In addition, the ability to measure is essential in successful CRM. This starts with the retailer creating the most relative metrics to measure the incremental impact of each marketing activity. A retailer can measure the value of sending an additional e-mail, the mailing of one additional direct mail piece, the mailing of the weekly circular, or spending an additional dollar for online display advertising.

Advanced analytics are key to determining the value of the media marketing mix. The combination of data mining, segmentation, predictive modeling, personalization, channel attribution, constant testing, and learning will enable the retailer to make fact-based decisions about marketing spend. A marketing executive was asked what most surprised him about his job. The answer? "I spent every day of the week working on the weekly circular." Analytics will enable executives to determine where their dollars and time are best spent.

Kroger is a leader in the grocery/supermarket sector when it comes to CRM. Its loyalty rewards card program allows it to track the behaviors of customers on more than 90 percent of in-store transactions. In terms of measurement, Kroger works with leading marketing analytics agencies to improve the marketing efficiency of cross-channel media campaigns via the latest attribution modeling techniques.

On the Horizon

A lot of the conversation around retail is focused on bricks-and-mortar stores versus online companies. A more relevant discussion, though, is on integration: providing an experience for the customer who does not separate those two modes of commerce. Successful retailers will be the ones who break down organizational silos, share a common customer framework, and provide a seamless omni-channel experience. The work begins at the current CRM maturity level, readiness, and passion. By applying a CRM approach, retailers can optimize how they use digital channels in combination with mass media to fully understand and know the marketing efficiency of every dollar spent.

Embracing this approach takes investment, time, and patience. However, the omni-channel customer experience will increase competitive advantage as customers continue to migrate to e-mail, online, social, and mobile applications to interact with retailers. Mobile is a particularly good opportunity, as studies have shown that once users start a purchase on their mobile phones, they will convert more often than when using other channels. Retailers need to employ mobile strategies to reach customers ahead of the competition, and early adopters will reap the rewards.

TRAVEL, MEDIA, AND ENTERTAINMENT

The State of CRM

The travel, media, and entertainment (TME) industry grouping consists of the travel brands: hospitality and lodging; airlines and rail; auto rentals; online travel agents and intermediaries; media companies, including broadcast, network, and publications; and entertainment companies, such as theme parks, production studios, and gaming. Across the spectrum of the TME industries, there are unique business objectives, yet they share a need to respond to similar market dynamics—changing customer expectations of the brand experience, increased competition for customer mindshare, and consumers' growing use of online tools and mobile devices throughout the purchase life cycle.

Iconic entertainment brands have been built on great guest experiences, and every customer touchpoint is an opportunity to fulfill the brand experience promise, whether it's previsit, on-site, or postvisit. However, although every touchpoint is an opportunity to reinforce the TME brand, because of the nature of the product or service itself, consumers *expect* their interactions with TME companies to be highly entertaining and personal.

A common characteristic across all three industries is the shared objective of getting more of the consumer's attention: in the case of media, more viewers and time spent viewing content; and for travel and entertainment, more share of the consumer's shrinking disposable dollar. To reach objectives, all three subverticals are placing a strong emphasis on delivering exceptional experiences—primarily across digital channels. To do so, TME companies need to get closer to the customer. However, it's worth noting that all three have varying business models and therefore face unique challenges in delivering a more customer-centric approach.

Furthest from the customer today, a media company's biggest challenge is becoming more customer centric with the ability to identify the customer across fractionalized media—traditional and online—combined with the challenge of "audience slide" (when customers control how they view media, such as over-the-top [OTT] programming such as Hulu or Netflix). Limited to subscription data to identify a segment of their customers, media companies have long relied on demographics (such as Nielsen) or a limited set of digital cookie data to further define the characteristics of their audiences. The challenge lies in the fact that they can't identify their customers on a one-to-one basis in order to attract viewers or visitors to content or recognize the viewer at every touchpoint. This effectively limits the ability to customize the experience or deliver personalized content to increase engagement or repeat viewership. Moving from the current state of having an anonymous audience to a known audience framework would allow media companies to push the most relevant content, better engage audiences, and, ultimately, optimize ad sales.

Entertainment companies are closer to the end customer, but they have the challenge of recognizing them at the beginning of the purchase cycle to influence purchase. For example, gaming companies know their customer at the time of game purchase, whereas theme parks know only segments of customers, such as season pass holders or customers who purchase before their arrival. The challenge is to leverage digital media and channels to move closer to the customer at earlier stages of the cycle, understanding the required value exchange between the customer and the brand to create more direct customer relationships.

Key to establishing these customer relationships earlier is the ability to identify the customer in the consideration phase. With the advent of technologies that allow more anonymous consumers to be identified, the entertainment industry can better understand the behavior that takes place as consumers are making decisions about how to spend their disposable income on entertainment options. This ability will enable the entertainment industry to offer more relevant options throughout the purchase cycle and across channels.

Travel companies have the business model that is closest to the customer and the most mature in terms of engagement tactics. With a loyalty-driven business model, travel brands know their customers at the point of purchase, such as when booking an airline ticket or reserving a hotel room. At this stage, customers must provide their personal information. Travel companies are pioneers in using loyalty programs as a means to further identify customers so that they can build customer engagement strategies and programs, and many industries have followed suit. Travel companies have also been pioneers in engagement tactics, with the development of apps and online resources to improve the customer experience. Flight reminders, notifications, destination suggestions, and concierge services are just a few examples of added customer value provided by a powerful app experience.

However, the challenge for travel companies lies in understanding how to spend dollars to reach the customers in the ways customers want to experience their brand interactions across more channels and media. For example, how should travel companies best interact with customers, and which segments of customers want new engagement tools such as mobile travel apps? Which media channels are most effective at attracting new customers? Although they may be closer to the customer, travel companies still lack the sophistication in attribution to best understand where to invest.

Industry Leaders Are Responding

Facing a range of challenges in getting closer to the customer, TME companies are employing several common strategies to become increasingly focused on customer centricity:

- *Delivering on expectations of the customer experience:* Obtaining competitive advantage requires the integration of multi-channel, media, and face-to-face customer experiences. Customer engagement models are becoming more real time, personal, and customized.
- *Digitizing, well, everything:* The explosion of digital media presents a wide range of opportunities to engage with customers. An increasingly digital environment also opens opportunities for data collection, insight generation, audience development, and multiple customer experience options.
- *Abandoning silos in brands, marketing, sales, and service:* Customer centricity is driving pressure within companies to abandon silos and integrate data, insights, and capabilities across the enterprise. This requires, in most cases, organizational transformation, a major challenge.
- *Embracing increasingly complex purchase cycles:* Customer purchase decisions continue to progress toward a highly iterative, social, and experience-based influence process. A customer-focused marketplace is driving the need for complex customer life cycle and moment-of-truth management.

On the Horizon

With a loyalty-focused business model, much like the retail industry, the TME industry in general is moving from an established customer-focused model to a higher level of sophistication with cCRM. Through cCRM, marketers can present customers with relevant products, content, offers, and information based on each customer's preferences. Those preferences can be known as a result of shared, observed, or derived data. cCRM produces personalization and informs the type of experience that should be delivered—a key ingredient in driving response, engagement, and repeat visits or purchases.

The cCRM goal of personalization for TME companies should be to integrate all customer attributes, behaviors, and preferences across channels into relevant and timely presentations of products, content, and brand information. Digital should be at the center of this focus. For example, e-mail click data can be incorporated into display ads and website landing pages for the promotion of a special event or offer, such as a film release or new video game launch. Social media interactions, search information, and all other online activities can drive relevant e-mail and direct mail messages. cCRM can incorporate all online and offline information about a customer, whether acquired directly from the customer or indirectly. For media companies specifically, the combination of offline and online data can better define the audience, drive content strategy, viewership, and sell more targeted media buys.

Although the personalization vision is shared by many companies in this industry, execution is challenging, from both an organizational and a resources perspective. Data integration, for example, requires an infrastructure that enables a holistic 360-degree view of the customer. It is essential to integrate demographic characteristics, transactional data (reservations, ticket purchases, etc.), online behavior (site, search, social, etc.), and customer preferences in an easy-to-use environment.

This integration is especially difficult when a company has different lines of business, brands, and different goals that drive marketing decisions. For example, some travel companies have separately run teams for their loyalty versus nonloyalty customers. Landing pages, content, and offers are generated separately for the two groups, with little integration. But what happens when a loyalty member searches anonymously? The experience can be vastly different and highly disappointing.

Ideally, organizations should be customer centric without lines that divide by channel, loyalty, or product. In a perfect end state, if a customer searches online for flights to Miami in October, a hotel and resort brand should be able to use display ads to target that customer for the right times and locations. Personalized landing pages can highlight the right destinations and use demographics and audience data to tailor content, price points, and specific amenities.

NONPROFIT

The State of CRM

There are currently more than 1.2 million nonprofit organizations (NPOs) in the United States. The marketplace is commonly broken into mission-focused subverticals, including international development and disaster relief, arts and culture, animal welfare and environment, education, health and healthcare, religious associations, and social service.

By definition, nonprofits are legally prevented from generating a profit and do not pay taxes. However, they do finance their work through positive net revenue generation programs with a substantive component coming via financial support from consumers—as individual giving. Individual giving to nonprofits was estimated at $223 billion in 2012, coming from 88 percent of U.S. households who gave an average of $2,213 each to nonprofits. Much like the for-profit sector, charities realize the need to develop deep relationships with their supporters, and they are dedicating significant time and funds to developing full (customer) donor life cycle programs. The programs are increasingly incorporating sophisticated acquisition and retention strategies, with particular sensitivity to understanding the unique engagement requirements of each generation in their donor base, including:

- *Silent generation:* A self-realized, traditional "give to help and to feel good" philanthropic generation who are currently the biggest givers by revenue. At 70 to 88 years of age, this generation is lucrative, but it represents a limited revenue pool, given current life expectancy rates.
- *Baby boomers:* The largest audience by donor count who are rejecting the silent generation's traditional philanthropic values, demanding real evidence of mission progress and demonstration of impact from their preferred charities. These 50- to 67-year-old donors are emerging as the most important constituents for many nonprofits.
- *Gen X:* The givers on the immediate horizon for most nonprofits, aged 30 to 50 years old, whose "worldview is based on change, on the need to combat corruption, dictatorships, abuse, AIDS, a generation in search of human dignity and individual freedom . . . and human rights for all."[6] This segment represents only a thin slice of revenues today and will require substantive fundraising program adaptation as the group ages up to the philanthropic sweet spot for nonprofits.

Today, nonprofits also contend with their enthusiasm for *new fundraising programs* and *new donor engagement channels*.

Industry Leaders Are Responding

Market-leading charities are expanding their audience reach by enlarging their fundraising program portfolio, augmenting foundational one-time giving and membership programs with segment-specific programs, such as gift catalogs, child sponsorship, peer-to-peer event giving, consumer-led crowdfunding, and increasingly, monthly giving programs. Managing a portfolio of giving "products" successfully delivers new donors and is common among top-notch charities. They do, nonetheless, struggle with the inherent portfolio management complexities: the need for strategic prioritization across the portfolio, accurate audience targeting within and across programs, budget allocation, data aggregation, hygiene and management, enterprise-wide reporting, and competing business unit goals that cause departments to work at cross-purposes even as they engage the same consumers.

Technology advances are spawning more donor engagement options, led by digital media, specifically search, display, social, and mobile advertising. In addition, technology-infused telemarketing is transforming via robocalls and other automated options, and TV advertising is getting more targeted with DRTV and the newest household-level targeting from cable and satellite providers. Street canvassing, door-to-door selling, retail merchandising, mall kiosks, and corporate-cause marketing further broaden nonprofits' fundraising reach. Leading groups are selectively investing in these channels even as they contend with the resulting integration challenges, which, for now, remain fundamentally unresolved for most groups.

Today, many nonprofit fundraising budgets skew (heavily) toward direct mail, an effective channel to engage the silent generation and to a lesser extent baby boomers. As they turn more and more to growing the next generations of donors—boomers and Gen X—who increasingly represent the bulk of individual giving revenue, nonprofits will need to focus on media and channels preferred by these digital media–savvy cohorts. This requires growing internal and external capabilities and capacity while also managing this shift to ensure that revenue growth aligns with investment.

This media and channel proliferation is increasing the need for nonprofits to become donor centric, with a small but growing contingent dedicating five- and six-figure budgets to cCRM.

Donor life cycle management is gaining attention within some development departments. For forward-thinking groups, there is a growing component of multi-department or multi-program donor segmentation that ties engagement to organizational strategy. Custom, segment-specific, targeted program elements (for example, creative, channel and media selection, contact frequency, and volume) are being validated via multi-month, structured test-and-refine plans.

Constituent data remain in silos. It is common to see many independent, decentralized, disconnected constituent data sources within a nonprofit, for example, separate e-mail, digital advertising, direct mail, and telemarketing databases. Data ownership is stratified with unique departmental stewards for each data source within a single organization. All of this continues to hinder nonprofits from assembling accurate, complete 360-degree views of supporters.

The solution to data silos—a focus on a central CRM database supporting strong data integration, data integrity, data enhancement, and data infrastructure with a single "view of the truth" or a single, shared snapshot of each constituent—is therefore widely recognized as a critical need by nonprofit executives. A few notable CRM database platforms are solidly contributing to the marketing success of a small number of groups, with a host of works-in-progress across the industry. A closer look inside these early adopters of CRM databases, however, reveals that the integral campaign management, business intelligence, and reporting tools have a limited reach, including some but not all of the key organizational business leaders.

Nonprofits routinely report encountering cross-departmental, cross-program, and cross-channel and media planning and decision-making friction. These challenges create less efficient fundraising programs, reduced revenue, and a weaker constituent experience. Despite wide recognition of this issue, only a small number of forward-thinking groups are investing in organizational assessment and road mapping initiatives to re-architect organizational structure, governance, and processes to support constituent-centric programs. There is real opportunity for growth and improvement in this arena.

On the Horizon

Nonprofit initiatives to broaden fundraising program portfolio management are under way, with significant growth and benefit expected over the next three to five years. They are moving from one-size-fits-all, campaign-based strategies to differentiated, optimized, portfolio approaches that maximize donor satisfaction and loyalty, as well as their value across programs and segments.

This move to microtarget communications, develop a 360-degree view of each constituent, and increase donor loyalty requires executive-level commitment within the organization and a sustained, well-funded investment strategy. As nonprofit vendors, media, and industry associations turn their efforts increasingly to this topic, we expect to garner more attention from charity board members and the C-suite, resulting in accelerated support for CRM.

Using analytics to garner an accurate measure of the impact of fundraising programs over time is a crucial component of CRM, providing necessary diagnostics and progress insights. Although *performance reporting* (How are we doing now?) and *projections* (Will we meet our future targets?) are common in the nonprofit industry, advanced analytics such as *attribution* (accurately assessing the contribution [value] of each constituent touchpoint) are primed for adoption in the next one to two years. Attribution will be essential for charities to understand the performance of each element of their expanding media and channel mix. Continued growth in other advanced statistical analysis, especially predictive modeling in content, contact, and offer strategy assessment and lifetime customer value projections will continue to accelerate as nonprofits deeply embrace data-driven decision making.

The macroeconomic outlook for the United States continues to improve and, with it, so does nonprofits' potential for individual fundraising growth and investment. Projections indicate that the next five years will see individual fundraising revenue regain prerecession levels.[7]

Who will win and lose during this rebuilding period?

> "The [Chronicle of Philanthropy] found that groups forecasting the best outlook for 2013 and beyond are those making innovations in how they attract gifts and diversifying their sources of revenue."
> —Blum and Hall, 2013

CRM programs that build a better constituent experience and grow donor loyalty while focusing on maximizing donor value across an expanding portfolio of fundraising programs and channels likely will see substantive gross and net revenue growth while outpacing their peers. This multi-year rebound will literally refashion the nonprofit landscape with smart investing and consistent organizational improvement as the fundamental differentiators between leaders and followers.

THINK VERTICALLY, ACT "UNIVERSALLY"

No matter where an organization lies on the customer-centricity continuum, by now we all agree that operating with a customer focus across all areas of the enterprise—and building customer value—are keys to success. The challenge, once there's "universal" buy-in on the philosophy, is the *how*. How do we successfully implement a comprehensive, data-driven, customer-centric business strategy? The answer is cCRM. The balance of this book will delve deeper into the philosophy of cCRM and the framework that supports it.

Chapter 4 Connected CRM

Building Customer Strategy as a Business Strategy

Our inspiration for developing the Connected Customer Relationship Marketing (cCRM) approach was not about a need to convince marketers that a customer-centric strategy is the path to business success. It was born out of the existence of a collective roadblock preventing marketers from following through on what they knew needed to be done. That roadblock represented the *how*—how to take customer centricity from an aspirational end state to a real way of life. cCRM is the way through the barriers. Instead of cringing at the increasing complexity of the marketplace, it allows brands to unveil the immense opportunity it creates. We define cCRM as "a systematic method of identifying, serving, and retaining customers based upon their value, through orchestrated customer interactions that improve financial results, create competitive advantage, and drive shareholder value." That's a mouthful, but when you break it down, you begin to see several distinct competencies that, once mastered, can drive competitive differentiation.

These competencies comprise a clearly rationalized framework that is at the heart of cCRM. It describes an ongoing process for complete enterprise implementation. Fundamentally, the approach is the same for every organization, with three seemingly simple steps: developing the strategy, building the infrastructure, and effecting the operational changes necessary to implement.

It's difficult. There are many aspects to consider. As soon as we start looking at CRM as a customer conversation as opposed to a media or campaign conversation, we have to take into account all these factors that influence the customer and the value associated with the customer. We see the framework in two dimensions. The capability dimension encompasses the development and mastery of competencies in the area of customer strategy, experience delivery, and financial management (Figure 4.1). The operating model dimension examines the core

The foundation of cCRM is a clearly rationalized strategic framework that is widely adopted at all levels of the organization and forms an ongoing process.

What data, processes, systems, tools, and technology will be necessary?

Infrastructure and Business Process

Enterprise segmentation, which includes value and life cycle dimensions, forms the foundation of the cCRM framework.

Customer Strategy

Portfolio Strategy

Segment Strategy | Program Strategy

These strategies are then translated into actionable media and channel plans that result in highly personalized, targeted experiences.

Experience Delivery

Media Planning | Channel Planning

Targeting and Personalization

Experience delivery performance is continuously attributed across media and channels, which, in turn, drives optimized budget allocation.

Financial Management

Measurement and Attribution

Budget Allocation

Financial management informs customer strategy and experiences delivery decisions as a closed-loop process.

Leadership and Organization

What outcomes are we trying to create, and how do we organize to enable them?

FIGURE 4.1 cCRM Framework

enablers of cCRM: infrastructure, process, organization, and leadership.

CAPABILITY DIMENSIONS

Customer Strategy

The first and arguably most important component of the cCRM framework involves the development of a strong customer strategy and vision for cCRM. But across industries, and even companies within industries, the definition of *customer strategy* can vary in scope: sales and service strategy, media strategy, brand strategy, customer experience strategy, contact strategy, digital strategy, content strategy—you get the picture. In reality, enterprise customer strategy encompasses all these things. In a customer-centric organization, customer strategy consists of a decision-making framework in which corporate-level assets are invested in the delivery of experiences across a portfolio of segments and customers. These experience investments have an expected economic return and have a direct impact on overall business performance.

A key word in that definition is *segments*. I fundamentally believe that successful customer strategy is rooted in world-class enterprise segmentation. Period. You simply can't do great customer marketing without honing those skills. The minute we can't identify every customer by name, we need another language through which to speak about and to those customers, a currency that the entire organization can understand and get behind. The idea that I can manage a portfolio of 30 million customers at an individual level just isn't practical, even in today's world. It's unfathomable. Everyone knows what segmentation is, and most have experimented with it. In practice, we have seen few brands that are able to create a segmentation capability that is truly "enterprise"—not used solely for targeting or limited to a particular point in time. Performed well, it is the primary currency by which the entire organization understands its customer sets. It sets the strategies, priorities, and investments associated with those customer sets. It separates the profitable customers from the unprofitable ones. It identifies the potential customers we want to work to win. And it's carried across all facets of the organization: the media strategy, channel strategy, product strategy, pricing strategy, promotion strategy, and so on.

Enterprise segmentation helps define how we link these strategies to customer value, which is the second critical currency of the customer strategy. If you don't have a customer value currency, I don't believe you can do effective customer marketing—and you certainly can't do effective integrated marketing, because you have no central construct within which to integrate. How would you ever make a decision to reallocate a resource from media A to channel B? You can't do it at the campaign level, because that's only one dimension. The only thing that matters is the ultimate value of that household or individual over time, how that value rolls up into the portfolio of customers, and how that creates growth, which, in turn, creates shareholder value.

Ultimately, good segmentation and value currencies are the two most powerful forces of a customer strategy. They feed the segment plan, or segment brief, which becomes a critical asset. The segment plan allows you to run well-executed campaigns, continuously evaluate those campaigns, and inform ongoing decisions about whom you want to reach, how and where to reach them, and the economic value that will be derived from those interactions. At the end of the day, week, or month, we can judge how we're performing against that predicted value.

A solid customer strategy enables improved lead generation, acquisition, cross-selling, and retention rates by delivering differentiated experiences consistently across all customer touchpoints. Brands can provide more relevant products, propositions, offers, and treatments. Purposeful portfolio strategy, including audience prioritization and personalization, leads to maximum return on marketing investment.

Experience Delivery

The next component of cCRM is about the way brands engage customers and customers engage brands. It involves identifying and effectively using the many online and offline, inbound and outbound touchpoints. From this comes the development of the capabilities required to manage those connections in an increasingly competitive environment.

In my years studying this marketplace, one of the things I've consistently found is that virtually nobody says a customer-centric strategy doesn't make sense, or doesn't apply to their industry or that they're not interested in becoming more customer focused. The snag comes when organizations start to try to define how they're going to get there. They know they should deliver personalized experiences, but what are those experiences actually going to be? The outlook can be overwhelming.

Within the experience delivery function, actionable consumer profiles are applied to perform targeting at the most granular available level, based on segment and individual-level characteristics: product preference, channel preference, propensity to respond, contact cadence analysis, and behavioral triggers.

The results of effective customer experience delivery are widespread and cumulative. Insight-driven targeting and rapid integration of learnings into ongoing and subsequent campaigns lead to higher response rates. Branded experiences that are differentiated yet consistent give rise to improved lead generation, acquisition, cross-selling, and retention rates. Minimizing the investment in lower-value customers results in improvements in both cost and profitability. Moreover, relevant customer experiences build engagement, loyalty, advocacy, and, ultimately, competitive advantage.

Financial Management

The third functional component of cCRM involves a broad measurement structure, which allows the organization to understand the relevant key performance indicators across the spectrum of customers, campaigns, media, channels, and so on. A strong financial management competency utilizes measurement and attribution techniques to enable media and channel budget application. It closes the loop, so to speak, from program execution to performance measurement and revenue attribution to use of the results to make better decisions about future program execution.

I've talked a lot about the big data explosion and the exciting insights it provides, which enable vast new targeting and personalization capabilities. The same excitement applies to measurement. There is so much change occurring in the ways we perform measurement and how we bring all the customer impressions, and their associated data, down to the consumer level. Our capabilities as marketers will continue to progress, giving us a much better understanding of the results our efforts are driving—and how they are interacting with one another.

Of course, for all the opportunity afforded by advancements in data, analytics, and technology, accurate measurement is still very difficult. Chief marketing officers (CMOs) still must justify marketing spend to chief financial officers (CFOs); they must allocate resources among TV, radio, print, e-mail, social, website, search, display, and other media and channels using information to inform those decisions.

Financial management must encompass a strong customer value currency and be conducted through measurement at the most granular level possible. Technology has allowed us to build superb measurement skill sets, which enable the study of customer event streams. From here, we can assign a specific behavior to a specific action or series of actions. These measurements inform budgeting and resource allocations, defining marketing mix analysis, forecasting, and planning to optimize results within each target segment.

Effective financial management provides a "true view" of campaign, program, and individual/segment performance as the foundation for decision making. The allocation of resources against well-defined CRM priorities will improve campaign and program results to increase the yield from media spend, maximize return on investment, and boost shareholder value. It is a difficult task, but these agile shifts in budget apportionment can really move the needle on business performance.

OPERATING MODEL DIMENSIONS

Infrastructure and Process

The first operating dimension of the framework, and overarching component of cCRM, is a comprehensive infrastructure, which encompasses the necessary systems, data, tools, and technologies that enable rich marketing activities across the cCRM framework. We see the connections between all the components as enterprise assets. The infrastructure is the part that makes all these functional areas of the framework real. For cCRM to thrive, a platform must be in place to physically make the connections between the media database, the customer database, the digital database, the prospect database, and so on, and organize that data to inform decisions. True integration of offline and online data across both anonymous and known identities enables organizations to create connected profiles that help rationalize customer identity and experience.

Ironically, it's not technology itself that limits our capabilities. It's often the organizational component that slows things down: information technology (IT), marketing, digital, even sometimes sales and finance owners are all buying pieces of technology. The difficulty is in developing the ability to link them all across those traditional silos.

The central construct of the infrastructure is the cCRM platform with a holistic architecture that can share insights to inform any marketing activity, whether it's a display advertising decision in real time or ongoing contributions to an optimization plan. It is based on a practical approach to cCRM capabilities that is scalable and flexible, adapting to dynamic environments. And it leverages repeatable components to accelerate time to market and realize swift but prolonged benefits.

Organization and Leadership

The second operational component of cCRM entails the organizational competencies required to enable the customer-centric transformation. It requires changes to leadership and management decision rights, changes to work groups and how they collaborate, and empowered top talent with the right incentives. When it comes to talking about matters of organizational change, people often slip into a state of denial, avoiding what can often be uncomfortable discussions about process, governance, human resources, compensation, and so forth. But this is one of the most critical components in a company's ability to get it right. In many ways, organization is a key driver of cCRM success.

At its core is leadership alignment around the CRM vision, with true sponsorship of the initiative and its financial commitments. Sponsorship must not be confused with permission. CRM is an executive-level commitment, which ensures that every functional area has a stake in the success of the effort. Work groups must be integrated to collaborate with one another, and the right talent must be in place and empowered with the right skill sets. Compensation must be properly aligned and enterprise-wide currencies in place to ensure success.

When all the disparate data finally begins to come together—and it will—organizational alignment will be one of the biggest challenges. But it's essential to the success of the CRM initiative. This preparation will help the company overcome traditional business silos with a focus on alignment of roles, responsibilities, and accountabilities. A commitment to building top talent relies on the right approach to hiring, training, and empowerment, especially with frontline personnel.

Ensuring success of any cCRM strategy requires swift but sustained proof of its value to the enterprise—and to the customer. Just as the implementation of the strategy itself must be carried out in a systematic, coordinated effort, so must the evaluation of its progress.

The central theme in the philosophy of building customer strategy as a business strategy is that successful change requires effective leadership. What makes change happen, and what could make it stall? Competitive advantage will be achieved by the ones who align their organizations—including executives, subsidiaries, departments, managers, staff, and partners—to effect fundamental and material change quickly and unflinchingly for the benefit of their shareholders, their customers, and, ultimately, themselves.

The following chapters will go into more detail about the five components of the cCRM framework. Mastery of these functional capabilities and their enabling competencies leads organizations to build customer strategy as a business strategy. I firmly believe the ultimate result will be sustainable competitive advantage.

Chapter 5 Customer Strategy

Creating Your Competitive Advantage

cCRM's AMBITIOUS GOAL

Connected customer relationship marketing (cCRM) is about integration, and that integration centers around a common construct: the customer. More than ever, building an enterprise-wide, customer-centric strategy that is able to drive investment decisions across the organization is critical to establishing sustainable competitive advantage.

Enterprise-wide, in this context, signifies that objectives are established from the top down and permeate all functions: customer and noncustomer facing. The traditional organization has not only allowed but expected customer-facing departments to establish their own customer strategy. Often I see companies that corner themselves into inconsistent customer treatment across the organization. For example, marketing staff may establish customer treatments based on their definition of customer priorities, whereas the call center team develops a set of tactics based on yet another set of independently defined customer priorities and the website team, acting autonomously, does the same (Figure 5.1).

All of these well-intentioned individuals in different departments are doing their best to deliver on a corporate goal (typically a product-centric goal). They recognize the need for some degree of customer centricity, but the lack of a top-down customer strategy requires these individuals to (1) concentrate on filling that void by creating their own customer strategy, resulting in redundant and often suboptimal efforts, and (2) divert attention from their true purpose: efficiently delivering on a strategy through, for example, best-in-class call center operations, leading-edge website interactions and personalization, and advanced digital acquisition programs.

Customer centric suggests that we must go beyond drawing insights and actually ensure that the customer expectations are profitably met in touchpoints across the organization. Targeted

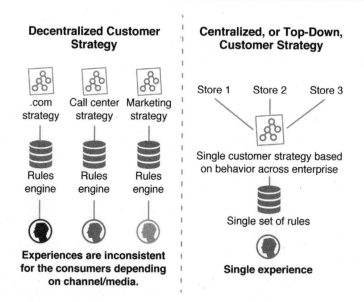

FIGURE 5.1 Centralized versus Decentralized Customer Strategy

customers must feel that the brand is for them and that the employees and processes are living the brand. What I am getting at here is that there must be a mutually beneficial relationship, and it's incumbent upon the company to define and cultivate that relationship better than and more efficiently than the competition. This requires several factors at the root of customer strategy:

1. *Customer portfolio management:* The organization must quantify consumers' real or expected long-term value to the company, determine how much to invest in the consumer, and then make tactical decisions accordingly (to ensure profitability).
2. *Segmentation:* The organization must understand consumers' expectations of the brand and category at large, which increasingly requires knowing more about the consumer than the consumers consciously know about themselves. This must be tied to customer economic value and behavior.
3. *Segment strategy:* For the organization to act in a unified manner, making coherent investment decisions and delivering a consistent yet differentiated experience, cCRM calls for an actionable and manageable way to embrace customer strategy.

CUSTOMER PORTFOLIO MANAGEMENT

Over the years, marketing has become increasingly relevant to executives, and I believe it's at least partially because its impact has become more measureable. However, marketing still lacks standard customer metric definitions tied to financial measures. Until the relationship between customer value and shareholder value is understood, defined, and commonly accepted, marketers will lack full pertinence in the boardroom.

Being strongly rooted in measurement, cCRM establishes that, should the primary function of a company be to create shareholder value, then the primary objective of marketers is to increase the value of customers. This implies that organizations have a responsibility to allocate investments in consumers (investment opportunities) to maximize profit while minimizing risk, a concept termed customer portfolio management.

Customer portfolio management, borrowing concepts from finance theory, suggests that by diversifying investments across multiple groups of customers with different risk/return profiles, a company can lower the risk that may be associated with investing in one group of customers. This may sound counterintuitive from an academic perspective, because as marketers we have been trained to think in terms of STP—segment target position, the idea that a company should rally around a target segment and build competitive differentiation to serve that segment. However, in today's highly complex environment, companies must marry laser-focused goals while simultaneously diversifying.

Let's take the mortgage industry as an example. Numerous financial institutions involved in the recent credit crisis assembled a portfolio of customers to maximize short-term returns but were willing to accept an inordinate amount of risk. A portfolio comprised only of high-income, wealthy individuals may have yielded a 4 percent return with minimal variance (risk), whereas one comprising only individuals with less accumulated wealth and lower income may have yielded an 8 percent return but with higher risk of loan default. In this example, evaluating the right mix of customers to maximize profit within the company's accepted risk tolerance would yield the optimal customer portfolio (given a set of defined constraints). Put another way, diversification of customers reduces exposure to individual assets (customers) in the portfolio.

Examples of risk that are prevalent in some industries but obscure in others include:

- Credit card and other lending institutions: risk of actual charge-off associated with individuals defaulting on a loan

- Insurance: risk of claims, which depending on the type of insurance, can include claims for medical matters, automobile accident, death, and home issues
- Travel: risk of cancellation of a reservation (we have seen airlines deal with this by assessing penalties)
- Medical: risk of adverse effect from the use of a product
- Other general services: risk of becoming a costly customer, that is, one who requires frequent touches through higher-cost channels

Like assessing any investment, evaluating customers or potential customers requires an adequate way to estimate the present value of future profit associated with that customer to determine how much a company is willing to invest to acquire the customer.

This is akin, in the financial markets, to valuing a company in order to estimate a reasonable share price. One would estimate future cash flow and then discount those cash flows back to a present value using a discount rate appropriate for the risk associated with the investment. Turning to corporate finance, we see that evaluating various projects would also entail estimating future value associated with a project, discounting that to a present value, and determining where to put precious investment dollars (when multiple investment opportunities present themselves), whether the hurdle rate is met, and ultimately whether the budget gets approved. Bringing this same rigor to cCRM, deciding which customers to invest in calls for multiple metrics:

- *Customer lifetime value (LTV):* This refers to the net present value (NPV) of future profit over the customers' expected lifetime (Figure 5.2). LTV is the primary measure of customer health and also informs how much a company is willing to invest in a customer (for example, offering differentiated treatment). More on this later in this chapter.

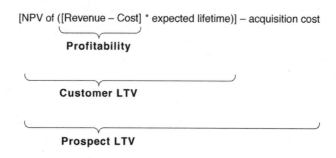

FIGURE 5.2   Customer Value Metrics

- *Profitability:* A critical component of customer LTV, profitability is revenue less costs associated with a customer for a specific time interval. Deconstructing profitability into revenue and cost allows executives to determine whether opportunities exist to increase revenue or decrease cost to serve.
- *Expected lifetime (referred to as survival):* This refers to the time period for which a customer is expected to endure. It is also a critical component of customer LTV; if LTV suffers and profitability is healthy, then the issue becomes retention. Defining a customer's expected lifetime is uniquely challenging in industries that lack contracts (such as consumer goods and retail).
- *Prospect lifetime value:* This is the expected customer LTV less acquisition cost. It informs decisions related to acquisition and also is sometimes referred to as customer equity or net customer profit because this metric takes into consideration the initial investment to acquire a customer.

These metrics are interrelated, and the underlying components boil down to estimating future revenue, future cost, expected lifetime, acquisition cost, and a discount rate based on information available now (that is, based on historical behavior; see Figure 5.2). Unique industry financial considerations, along with the corporate business models, affect how we address value. And although revenue drivers are typically widely known and accepted, costs are often a subject of debate.

For MetLife, expected customer value is based on profitability and expected lifetime. Profitability calculations include actual revenue (the premium) less costs, such as reserves that are set aside in the insurance industry, service overhead (informed by finance), and post-acquisition costs such as payment processing. Survival modeling based on historical data and product owner-ship (for example, number of policies, length of term) is used to determine the expected relationship duration. These metrics are used to evaluate the attractiveness of prospects by developing a predicted customer value and marrying that with expected acquisition costs, including marketing costs, sales commissions, medical exams, and underwriting costs.

Another excellent example of value analysis comes from one of our technology clients, which was able to identify the minority of consumers contributing a majority of value to the company; the consumers who destroy value were identified as well (Figure 5.3). This view of individual consumer value in terms of contribution to overall corporate value enables

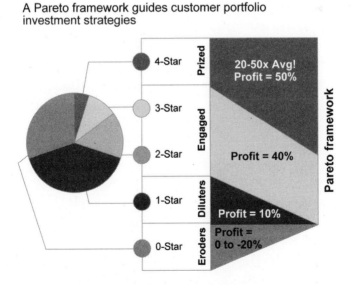

A Pareto framework guides customer portfolio investment strategies

FIGURE 5.3   Pareto Principle

strategic decision making by treating each customer as an individual project to be evaluated or stock share to be assessed for inclusion in the portfolio.

I mentioned earlier that customer LTV is a measure of customer health and that to become increasingly pertinent in the boardroom, marketers must demonstrate financial relevance. Expanding on that, one can conclude that LTV is, or should be, correlated with overall market value. Gupta, Lehmann, and Stuart examined data from multiple companies to show that customer LTV may provide a good proxy for corporate value.[1] Another study showed that customer LTV is highly correlated with corporate value using a longitudinal analysis.[2] This is not surprising given that increased customer value translates into accelerated and enhanced cash flow and reduced volatility in earnings.

I also mentioned earlier that customer LTV informs investment decisions. From a customer base perspective, LTV is the forerunner of differentiated treatment. Considering the lifetime or survival rate and the profitability of customers has bearing on objectives related to those customers (Figure 5.4).

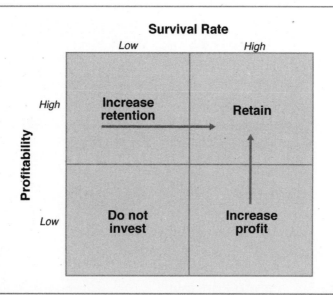

FIGURE 5.4 Survival Rate and Profitability

ENTERPRISE SEGMENTATION

Until this point, my colleagues entrenched in database marketing should be nodding their heads at the familiarity of the concepts introduced. It was those database marketers who spent years convincing organizations that needs drive behaviors, behaviors drive value, and therefore, to impact value, what was historically brand budget (mass media) must be reallocated to direct marketing. They focused religiously on direct marketing profit drivers (audience, offer, creative, message, channel, contact) to generate lift based on behavioral and value segments, proving that marketing is, in fact, measurable and that by understanding behavior, it can be influenced.

Simultaneously, other departments at the same enterprise would develop "strategic" segments. These would be groups such as "women," "Hispanics," or persona-based segments such as "innovators" and "traditionalists," serving as inspiration for new strategic targets. Beyond personas, the traditional agency approach is to conduct research using a relatively small sample of data, draw rich insights, and use typing tools to assign other individuals to those segments in the future. The flaw lies in the fact that unless given the opportunity to ask the typing tool questions, the organization has no idea which segment an individual falls into, limiting actionability.

At the same time, other more tactical segmentation schemes arise. Sales leaders think of markets they can assign to their teams. Channel leaders think of new websites they can develop for unique audiences. Product marketers think of customer programs they can launch to drive program uptake. And customer care leaders think of ways to reduce handling time for those stubborn callers who just won't hang up. In reality, all these business challenges and opportunities can be informed by segmentation, but few companies have invested in developing a segmentation capability that can address them all. This is why companies frequently have numerous segmentations that address an isolated business issue. Sometimes they are effective but struggle to reach a common definition of the consumer, generate deep consumer insights, and act on them consistently across the organization (Figure 5.5). That's what has to change.

Enterprise segmentation aligns the business around a common customer strategy and shared vernacular, threading together rich strategic insights on prospects and customers while maintaining tactical relevance (Figure 5.6).

Multiple dimensions of insight comprise enterprise segmentation:

- *Motivational insights:* Deep-rooted motivations, along with personal experiences and outside influences (e.g., friends, advertising), affect attitudes and needs, which in turn drive behaviors that create or destroy value (Figure 5.7). To appeal to and motivate consumers, we must recognize their underlying motivations. Motivations help answer the why of consumer behavior.
- *Customer value:* Overlaying customer value on motivational segments helps marketers identify micro-segments, which in

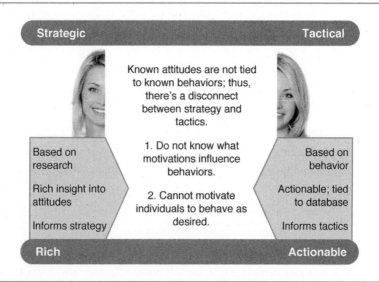

FIGURE 5.5   Multiple Segmentation Schemes

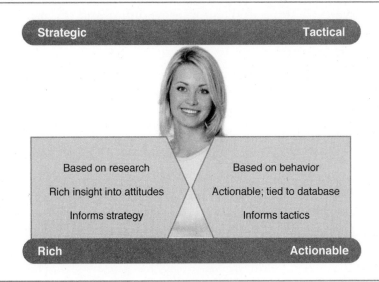

FIGURE 5.6   Enterprise Segmentation

turn help them make the optimal investment decisions described in the preceding portfolio section.

- *Behavioral insights:* Because behavior is a key link between motivations and value, it is an important component of implementing enterprise segmentation, particularly because it is that very behavior we want to influence. Behaviors are typically

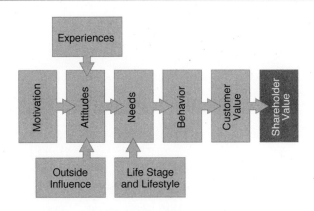

FIGURE 5.7   Motivational Insights

observed (via data) and can refer to online and offline actions, although self-reported behavior helps marketers understand noncustomers.

- *Other insights:* Other insights into segments, which don't necessarily drive the actual segments but offer a richer understanding of them, are attitudes, needs, psychographics, demographics, media usage, brand relationships, and share of wallet (more on these later in this chapter).

My context here is that *the number one goal of an organization is to motivate behaviors that drive value.* So studying and measuring value and understanding customers are critical to developing an actionable customer strategy as a business strategy.

Acting on the strategy is discussed extensively in the coming chapters. We will address life cycle marketing, the role of demographics, and propensity and response models in targeting, tailoring experience based on preference. This all matters, but first an organization must have a customer strategy in place.

Inherently, enterprise segmentation must fill the needs of multiple stakeholders in the organization. An organization must ask itself what those needs are:

- *What is the market I'm trying to segment?* The answer to this deceptively simple question varies based on industry and corporate dynamics. Generally speaking, it is superior to look not just at customers alone but also at the broader marketplace so as not to fall victim to what Merkle calls the targeting dilemma. What we mean by that is that marketers have become very adept at taking a value proposition and finding people who want to buy it. The dilemma is that we're not as good at understanding our audience's behaviors and tailoring value propositions to meet their needs. Think about it: As you get better at targeting, you're eliminating what may or may not have been waste. You're narrowing your universe and driving traffic, but not growth. There is no way to reverse that tendency without segmentation. Let's consider two examples:

- ○ When MetLife's Direct Distribution team came to us for segmentation support, they had been targeting the life insurance "middle market," a younger-than-45-years-old population. Studying their customer base would lead to a targeting dilemma: a belief that the younger-than-45 population is the most relevant population for MetLife. The company would try to build more campaigns to take advantage of the opportunity, unaware of the broader marketplace opportunities. Rather than studying only the customer base, we studied the general marketplace and identified a number of untapped segments to explore.

- ○ A company restricted to certain geographies would most likely benefit from a regional study; however, in the early 2000s Cingular Wireless had network capacity only in certain areas, yet understanding the broader marketplace (regardless of geography) would be important in helping prioritize network rollout. A broader, rather than narrow perspective, in this case, allows an enterprise view.

- *What challenges am I solving?* Again I encourage thinking broadly yet thoroughly. Remember that enterprise segmentation mobilizes the organization around a common customer lens and must flex to support multiple, maybe many, functions; it also must be actionable (meaning that down-the-line tactics informed by segmentation need to be understood before completing segmentation efforts).

Figure 5.8 depicts the most common areas for explorations. Our fundamental approach to understanding motivations and valuing customers does not change based on these requirements; however, the priority of the different applications affects:

- The specific context of those motivations. For example, a company determining whether to expand from selling women's clothing to also selling accessories and personal items will need to understand motivations differently than a company

Corporate Strategy	Customer Strategy and Marketing Mix
• Market sizing	• Product road map, positioning, and assortment
• Brand positioning	• Price/offer strategy for product
• Strategic targeting	• Channel strategy
• Investment decisions	• Media budget allocation
• Corporate financial goals	• Desired experience (the "feel")
	• Value proposition

Program Decisions
Messaging · Contact cadence · Offers · Creative · Measurement and attributes

FIGURE 5.8   Areas for Exploration

deciding whether to expand its line from high-priced goods to more affordable goods.

- The types of descriptors needed to portray segments. For example, a primarily online company may focus on profiling segments with data on online behavior, whereas a brick-and-mortar outfit would need to understand the consumers' buying process along with in-store expectations.

Enterprise Segmentation: Understanding Motivations

To influence marketing decisions, we must first understand decision-making processes, so we turn to consumer behavior models. Thought leadership on consumer decision making has emerged from economic and psychology disciplines, combining the quantitative aspects of economic models (the assumption that consumers have perfect information and act rationally) with the qualitative aspects of psychological and cognitive models (examining motivations and needs).

My belief is that consumers make purchasing decisions not simply because of the product features but because those features

Personal Values	Why valued emotions are important to us *Example: Safety links to my value of family security.*
Emotions *Psychosocial Consequences*	The emotional benefits of the functional benefits *Example: Good cell service makes me feel safe.*
Benefits *Functional Consequences*	The positive aspects of the attributes, why they are important *Example: The service and call quality are good.*
Brand/Product Attributes	The things directly associated with the product or brand *Example: The mobile provider guarantees no dropped calls.*

FIGURE 5.9   Consumer Decision Making

provide benefits that resonate with personal values (Figure 5.9). Most research does not address the personal values, falling short of answering why consumers make the decisions they do.

To illustrate, the mappings depicted in Figures 5.9 and 5.10 are adapted from a recent project for a major home improvement retailer. Traditional market research would focus on the brand/product attributes and benefits (the bottom two layers of the diagram) but not address the more personal (higher in the map) aspects.

By connecting brand attributes to brand benefits and then to emotional consequences and personal values, we gain insight into the underlying human motivations and the related decision-making process. Like traditional research, a qualitative approach is used to map out the consumer decisioning process; quantitative research then validates these "chains" and, more important, tells us which chains are most relevant to specific individual survey responders.

The implications of this research are wide reaching. Understanding decision-making processes makes enterprise segmentation relevant:

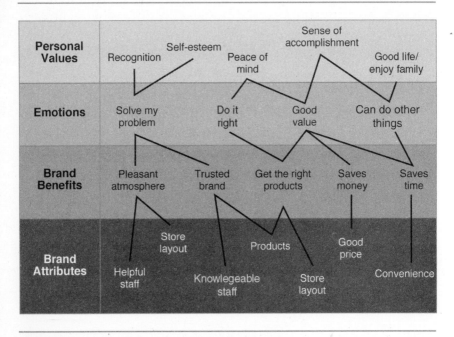

FIGURE 5.10 Consumer Decision Map

- Brand and mass advertising benefit from insights into needs, attitudes, and product/brand benefits perceived, enabling richer positioning and messaging.
- Product teams benefit from the linkage between features, functional benefits, and emotional implications, which inform product development.
- Sales and service can design offerings based on values (such as peace of mind versus sense of accomplishment) to ensure differentiated treatment.

Enterprise Segmentation: Creating the Segments

As mentioned previously, a data collection effort occurs to tie individuals to decision-making chains. The survey includes a very specialized set of questions, as well as questions that will be used to describe the segments. This brings us back to the importance of determining enterprise-wide uses of segmentation early in the effort. Survey design, sampling, and execution are sophisticated and require many considerations. The topic has been studied and written about extensively; yet for this book, I want to highlight cCRM's value beyond what many readers are already familiar with. So, although the topic is significant, I will skip many of the details related to data collection.

The segmentation process itself achieves two core objectives: identifying groups of consumers (for example, survey responders) who share decision-making chains and projecting those common groups on the larger population of prospects and customers (referred to earlier in the chapter as mapping).

Groups of customers with shared decision-making chains become your segments. As a simplified example, let's say that through various analytical techniques, a retailer finds that two market segments exist. One seeks an optimal store layout and selection, because it ultimately drives peace of mind. Another seeks deals and promotions, because it links to the feeling of accomplishment (Figure 5.11). Typically, there are multiple solutions from an analytical standpoint, so business reviews cannot be overlooked when identifying the optimal solution.

The typical attitudinal segmentation stops here or, if any mapping occurs, results in a 30 to 50 percent accuracy. A segmentation solution with such little reliability raises concern.

We approach mapping differently. Rather than relying on a typing tool, which allows segment assignment only of those who respond to the typing tool questions, and then projecting the solution to the database based on personas, we append survey data with individual-level data that is available on all prospects and/or customers and then develop analytically rigorous models to assign segments (Figure 5.12).

The last step is merging the segmentation study data to the same set of data so that the final segment descriptors can be based on the one-to-one linking rather than an aspirational persona (Figure 5.13).

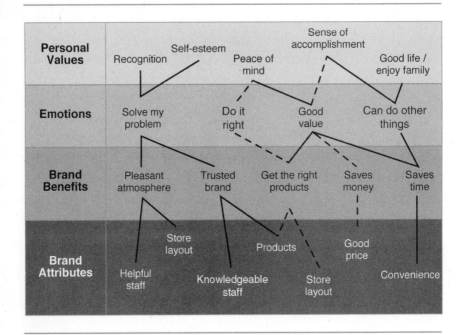

FIGURE 5.11 Relevant Consumer Decision Chains

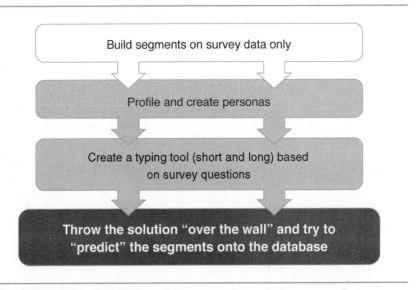

FIGURE 5.12 Traditional Approach to Segmentation

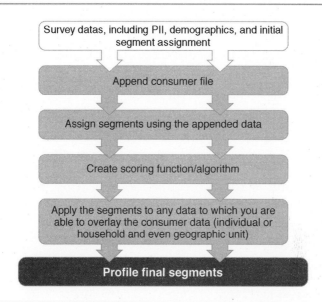

FIGURE 5.13   cCRM Approach to Segmentation

This concept may sound incredibly simple, but its importance is vast. By tying the segments to the entire population, we are enabling cCRM.

Enterprise Segmentation: Describing the Segments

Segment coloring, as it's often called, leverages survey data, data in the database, and other third-party information to create the richest profiles possible. The survey portion must be carefully considered before launch, and the rest is enabled through name and address matching. The coloring varies based on the business context, but consistent themes surface (beyond the decision-making chain).

A traditional profile summarizes findings, but to be actionable, it must be much deeper. It is therefore imperative that segmentation within an organization drive the profiling.

- *Industry-specific attitudes and needs:* Study feelings and thoughts about the brand, product, and/or services that comprise the industry. These attitudes are best understood through examples: Responders may be asked how much they agree with statements such as "I am very interested in pet products," "My pet is part of the family," "I want my pet to be an extension of me," and "When looking for pet care products, I do my research."

- *Psychographics:* Personality, values, and interests admittedly overlap some of the values mentioned earlier; however, psychographics are more general in nature, rather than specific to an industry. This data can be purchased or included in the study and include agreement levels on statements such as "I am risk averse," "I am usually the first of my friends to try something new," "My family is the most important thing to me," and "I shop for deals."

- *Demographics:* Demographics used to be important for targeting, but these days more sophisticated solutions exist compared with those available even just 10 years ago. Demographics do provide a sense of the audience at hand. Because we typically append data to survey responder data, inclusion of demographic questions in a survey is minimal, except to the extent that we need to use those questions to manage survey responder volumes and ensure proper sampling.

- *Media usage:* Media usage and insights are critical to executing on segment strategy. Understanding what media (TV, radio, print, outdoor, digital) are used, as well as more specifics, such as what TV networks, radio programs, specific publications, and specific properties are consumed, is also important. Top properties are available via syndicated tools, but industry specifics may be helpful to ask about. We have been successful in integrating segments into media planning tools by working with syndicated data providers as well.

- *Brand relationships and share of wallet:* This includes soft metrics such as questions around awareness, consideration, relevance, and likelihood to recommend, as well as evaluation of brand attributes associated with various companies. Monetary metrics, such as share of wallet across brands and intended spend by brand, can be important in understanding the real monetary opportunity associated with segments.

- *Behaviors:* In this context, *behaviors* refer to the self-reported ones; for example, "Have you shopped for insurance?" "What prompted you to shop?" "How did you do your research?" and "Have you purchased and why or why not?" Although not as powerful as demonstrated behavioral data possessed at a company (such as transactions or website searches), this data provides insights into other behaviors that a company can't track (such as activity with other brands).

- *Input to experience mapping:* This is one of the most difficult areas to plan for and the most variable by industry. For this, one must have a high-level understanding of various touchpoints and the levers that can be pulled at each one to deliver a more relevant experience.

- *Value:* Insights into the value components of each segment further enrich understanding of churn/retention, profitability, and acquisition cost. Much more than just profiling is needed, but I would be remiss to omit mention of value here.

PORTFOLIO STRATEGY: UNITING THE SEGMENTATION SCHEME WITH PORTFOLIO OPTIMIZATION

The interplay between attitudinal or motivational segments and customer portfolio optimization, although referenced sporadically thus far, is vital to a sound segment strategy. Sometimes referred to as micro-segmentation, pulling together a consolidated view of attitudinal or motivational segments and value analysis incites the segment-specific strategies comprising the overall customer (cross-segment) strategy.

First, we observe potential opportunities by examining the overall market potential and the sales and marketing funnel, in

	Movers & Shakers	Family Matters	Mature Planners	Passives	Loners
% of U.S. Population	20%	20%	30%	20%	10%
% of Leads	15%	30%	10%	25%	20%
% of Customers	30%	30%	20%	10%	10%
Value	High	Medium	High	Low	Low

FIGURE 5.14   Funnel Analysis

this example, the segment composition of the U.S. population, MetLife leads, and MetLife customers. I'll use camouflaged segment names, descriptions, and numbers to protect any proprietary or strategic information. (See Figure 5.14.)

Overall market potential is best gleaned through a combination of primary and secondary research, which tells us that more than 35 million uninsured or underinsured households, half of whom say they are ready to buy, exist in the United States, translating into billions of dollars in revenue. Looking at the segments comprising the broad market, we learn that two of the segments tend to be (1) uninsured or underinsured, having minimal coverage now and often having dependents, and (2) open to the idea of insurance. These are the Movers and Shakers and Family Matters segments. Based on the study elements on wallet share mentioned earlier, we also have a view of market share, allowing us to set market share goals for these two segments.

Funnel analysis indicates that Movers and Shakers are the highest value segment, accounting for 20 percent of the U.S. market but only 15 percent of leads and 30 percent of customers. Based on those percentages, it can be concluded that marketing is not targeting Movers and Shakers now. The sales process resonates well with Movers and Shakers, as evidenced by the fact that the segment converts well (comprising 15 percent of leads but 30 percent of customers). In contrast, a low-value segment, the Loners segment, comprises 10 percent of the market and 20 percent of leads, suggesting that marketing may be targeting a low-value, low-conversion segment.

We have established that there are opportunities to better target the Movers and Shakers through lead generation and acquisition campaigns. Looking more closely at Movers and Shakers comprising the existing customer base, we see that 30 percent have a low lapse rate but also low profitability, indicating that the organization should focus on growing earnings from this group through cross-selling or up-sell initiatives. Another 40 percent are highly profitable and tend to renew; this group should be rewarded for their loyalty. The 20 percent of the base that is profitable but lapses at a higher-than-average rate reflects a retention issue. (See Figure 5.15.)

In contrast, those in the Family Matters segment, 30 percent of the leads, are entering the funnel and converting at an average rate. (We know this because they comprise 30 percent of leads

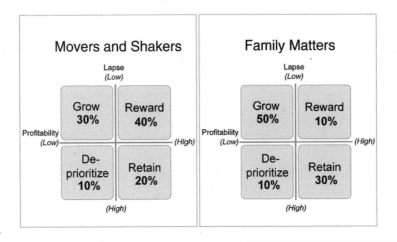

FIGURE 5.15   Segment-Specific Strategy

and 30 percent of customers.) Of course, we could share actual conversion rates, which would tell the same story. As we concentrate on the Family Matters segment, we learn that the biggest opportunity among this group is to increase the LTV or grow premium to drive greater customer value.

The organization must determine where to put its investment. A business case accounting for various components informs decisioning:

- *Acquisition:* addressable market size, expected customer value, expected cost to acquire
- *Retention:* initiative cost, expected incremental retention
- *Growth:* initiative cost, expected incremental profitability based on cross-sell potential and product profitability
- *Reward:* initiative cost, risk of not investing in reward

A very simplistic view illustrates that this approach yields insights on priorities. In practice, multiple evaluation criteria are taken into account, including:

- Shareholder value (informed by profit) created over specific time horizons relevant to the company (for example, 1- or 2-year time frames)
- Customer equity, which takes a longer-term view because it considers LTV (or profit over the long term) less investment cost
- Return on investment (ROI)/internal rate of return (IRR) on various projects because the company must ensure that investments clear existing hurdle rates

For clarity's sake, though, let's accept that the organization will invest in increased acquisition of Movers and Shakers and growth and retention of the Family Matters segment because the greatest opportunity, based on MetLife's evaluation criteria, lies there (Figure 5.16). Now what?

	Movers and Shakers	Family Matters
Increase Lead Volume	$$$	NA
Grow	$$	$$$
Reward	$	$$
Retain	$	$$$

FIGURE 5.16   Valuing the Strategy

SEGMENT STRATEGY

Aligning the organization around the newly prioritized segment objectives that comprise the portfolio strategy means mobilizing the troops and arming them with a vision and strategy for each segment—but with unwavering support of the brand strategy that encompasses the company's identity and value proposition. Chapter 9 will explore this balancing act in more detail.

I suspect that businesspeople would have a fairly common reaction if asked what a product strategy entails. They may cite product penetration goals, market share goals, development road maps, marketing, sales and service strategies, and so on. A customer segment strategy consists of similar components. The penetration and market share equivalents were mentioned earlier, so this section describes the marketing, sales, and service strategy that cCRM must contemplate.

Marketing aspects of the segment strategy gain inspiration from the 4 Ps: product, price, place (distribution), and promotion. Products to address current and untapped needs must be evaluated, and those products must be viewed through a segment lens. For instance, product managers typically have overall objectives, but with the micro-insights that segmentation yields, product managers' views must shift as well. Another way of saying this is that a product manager may typically ask, "Who is the target audience for my product?" but they should be thinking, "What products do I need to build and manage to satisfy a segment's personal values and decisioning processes?" The measurement mind-set shifts as well—product penetration, average number of products per consumer, revenue per product, margin per product, and overall product contribution are still relevant, but they must be scrutinized by segment (Figure 5.17).

Pricing concepts and strategy similarly exist at a segment level. Pricing strategies abound (for example, cost plus, skimming, loss leader), and much has been written on the topic. These strategies are valid and tested, and the concepts are unchanged, except that they must be applied to each segment differently. Similarly, promotion and offer strategies could be studied in traditional manners through market research or in-market testing. Finally, price sensitivity can be gauged through research, asking about attitudes on price, as well as through more scientific means, as illustrated in Figure 5.18, which we have used with retail clients. We have successfully identified for different motivation segments optimal price points though price sensitivity meters.[3] The basic premise is that certain price points are too expensive to convey value, whereas others are too low to convey quality.

Distribution and promotion strategies are inherently driven by the strategic nature of enterprise segmentation. A premium brand can uncover opportunities to address different markets through alternative distribution channels. For instance, MetLife began a pilot program to distribute products through Walmart in 2012, allowing for greater reach into previously untapped segments, acting on MetLife's vision to make life insurance available to everyone. Consumer goods companies, which typically command higher margins, can vastly expand their distribution volume by entering into partnerships with large-scale retailers such as Costco, a strategy that requires a reexamination of not only distribution but also product and price point considerations.

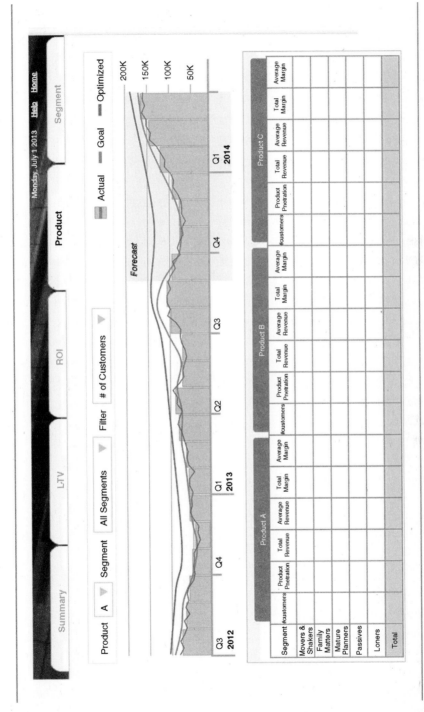

FIGURE 5.17 Tracking Performance

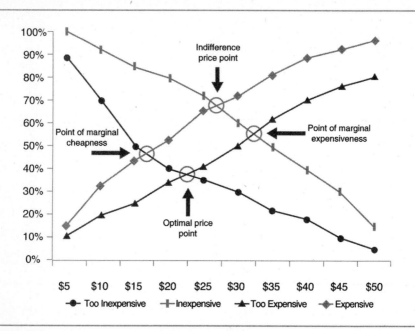

FIGURE 5.18   Price Sensitivity Meter

Finally, sales and service can be vastly affected by enterprise segmentation, because investment priorities, as well as the desired segment experience, make a difference. Decisions around priorities rely primarily on value metrics: higher-value or higher-potential-value customers receive more expensive treatment, such as being prioritized in the interactive voice response (IVR) system, given sweeter retention offers, and so on. The experience designed is born from segment-specific expectations of the brand and the personal values uncovered during primary research studies.

We recently worked with a major regional bank whose insights into existing customers helped launch its customer experience mapping effort, where differentiated treatment by segment, based on both value and motivations, were designed.

Through experience mapping (Figure 5.19), I've seen companies deliver more relevant digital interactions, lead-nurturing communications, and call scripting. Database marketers have

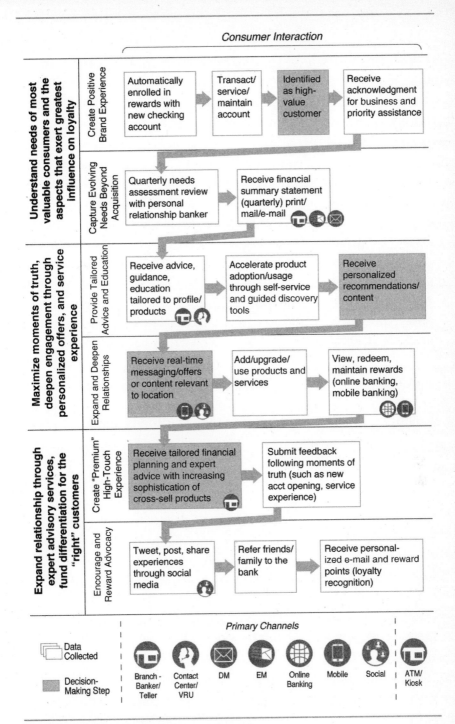

FIGURE 5.19 Experience Mapping

known for years how to determine the next best offer, average handle time goals based on value of the customer, and the like. Now, with enterprise segmentation, we also have a tool to shape purely experiential actions, because we can tie an individual to a motivational segment.

A deliverable called the segment brief is the culmination of the market, sales, service, and product strategies described. The brief is the one-page guide (with a large body of analysis and deliverables supporting it) that rallies the organization around a cross-functional, enterprise view of the customer. It is most effective as a brochure (pictured) or as a grid describing the segment in terms of sales, service, marketing, and product priorities related to investment, messaging and positioning, and experience/feel desired to deliver a consistently differentiated set of treatments.

CUSTOMER STRATEGY: OTHER CONSIDERATIONS

Customer strategy is not stagnant. The many tendrils of customer strategy require tracking, measurement, and refinement enterprise-wide. This concept, although reinforced throughout this book, deserves additional mention, for a customer strategy is only as powerful as its adoption, care, and feeding. This means that new processes must be developed, infrastructure enhancements may be needed, and surely organizational changes should be contemplated. Although these concepts are covered elsewhere in this book, I will take a moment to introduce the importance of a segment evangelist, who in theory has support from segment stewards. The job description in Figure 5.20 was written tongue-in-cheek, but it reveals the brutal truth of what is needed to be successful.

Customer strategy, although blatantly logical, does require a shift in thinking about the role of channel and product within organizations; hence, the mention of segment stewards (or segment managers should an organization be more aggressive

Wanted:

Sharp, thick-skinned, evangelical marketer skilled at organizational change and able to help one of the world's most respected brands become more customer centric. Within one year you will permeate a deep understanding of our customers (segments) across our organization. You will create and lead a portfolio of programs that generate applause-worthy gains across customer touchpoints. You will improve the way we design, deliver, and talk about our products. If you succeed, thousands of lives will be changed for the better.

Success is not guaranteed. Most customer-centricity efforts fail because companies can't translate their insights into action or don't get buy-in from the people who can effect change. You will face these same obstacles. You will deal with time-pressured peers who want to listen but have their own priorities. You will at times feel stuck, limited by legacy technology and a slow-moving organizational culture. But you will not be alone. In your corner will be a top-notch marketing agency and a senior executive team that is actively engaged and on your speed dial.

Responsibilities:

- Coordinate efforts across the organization to maximize relationships with its customers
- Define and drive acquisition, development, and retention goals at the business and customer-segment level
- Work with product and media/channel owners to deliver on segment objectives
- Develop and maintain corporate vision of customer centricity as it relates to the direct distribution channel segments
- Engage stakeholders, manage buy-in, and provide creative solutions to roadblocks
- Build an organization to deliver customer centricity; manage segment-specific resources
- Define and support delivery of appropriate inbound and outbound customer experience (phone, Web) for different segments. Work with your team to build hypotheses, develop tests, mine data, and draw insight
- Engage management team in a dialog around this program and customer segments in general
- Apply an analytical, hypothesis-driven approach to marketing
- Design and execute market research

Experience/Skills/Knowledge:

- Experience leading change
- Record of using data and analytics to drive successful marketing programs
- History of establishing a vision for the customer experience
- Delivered insights to colleagues in strategic and operational functions
- Successfully delivered acquisition, development, and retention goals using CRM marketing principles
- Strong personal brand complemented by operational know-how
- Ability to build alliances

FIGURE 5.20 Perfect Candidate for Customer Strategist

with its path to cCRM Nirvana). To demonstrate what a segment manager does, I reiterate that *the number one goal of an organization is to motivate behaviors that drive value.* Thus, it's only logical that someone be accountable for this ambitious goal, managing segments as most organizations manage products or brands.

What does a segment manager care about? To answer this question, let's turn to Figure 5.21, a snapshot of a segment dashboard. Such a dashboard gives managers the tools to track the most important metrics, such as LTV, ROI, and media and product contribution. If you can build one report and only one report related to your segments, look at the bottom left table in this dashboard. It displays the tracking of a motivational segment by value tiers so that a segment manager can see where value migration is occurring (for example, for my Movers and Shakers segment, what percentage increased their LTV since the prior period, what percentage decreased, and what percentage stayed the same?).

FROM BASIC CAPABILITIES TO HIGH PERFORMANCE

This chapter started off with "cCRM's Ambitious Goal." It's important to note that a strong customer strategy evolves as part of a journey with an ambitious end state and continuous improvement. Of the many brands I've worked with, I have seen a continuum of sophistication upon which capability and operating model maturity evolves. Not all companies need to be a level 5 (highly mature) to be successful (Figure 5.22). Rather, for the highest ROI, one could argue that it's best to achieve optimization at the lowest possible level of maturity to retain competitive advantage.

One of the most difficult lessons marketers can learn is that, in the quest for optimization, not every prospect can be converted and not every customer can be retained. In fact, that notion goes against the very definition of customer centricity. Michael

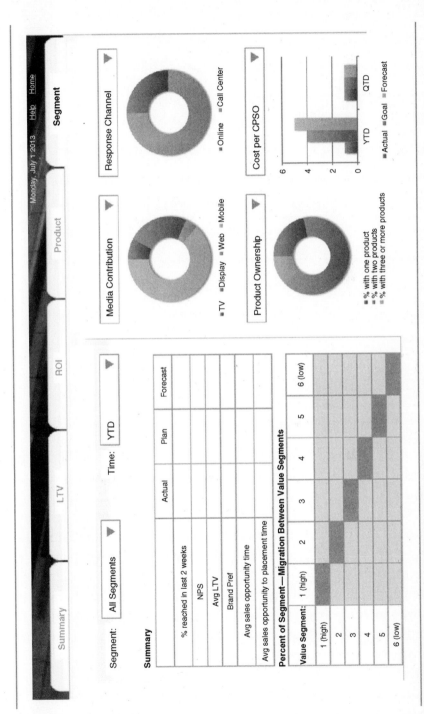

FIGURE 5.21 Segment Dashboard

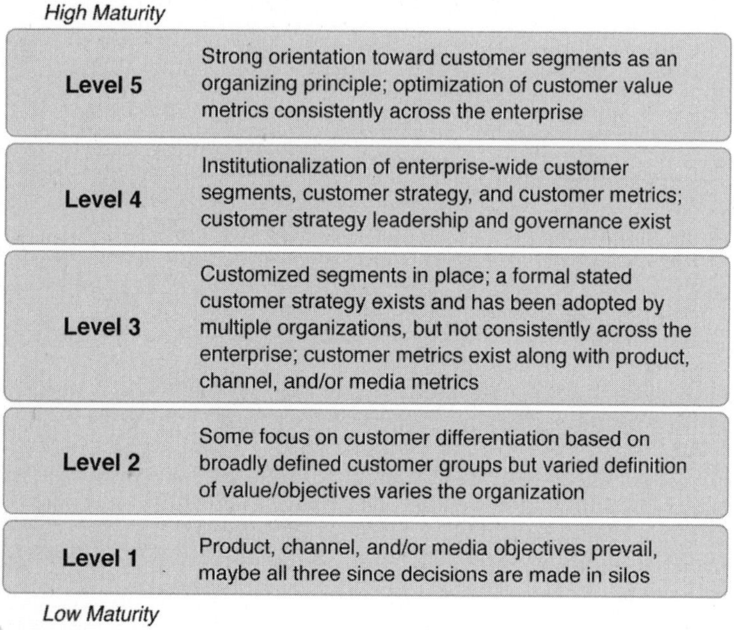

High Maturity

Level 5	Strong orientation toward customer segments as an organizing principle; optimization of customer value metrics consistently across the enterprise
Level 4	Institutionalization of enterprise-wide customer segments, customer strategy, and customer metrics; customer strategy leadership and governance exist
Level 3	Customized segments in place; a formal stated customer strategy exists and has been adopted by multiple organizations, but not consistently across the enterprise; customer metrics exist along with product, channel, and/or media metrics
Level 2	Some focus on customer differentiation based on broadly defined customer groups but varied definition of value/objectives varies the organization
Level 1	Product, channel, and/or media objectives prevail, maybe all three since decisions are made in silos

Low Maturity

FIGURE 5.22 / Maturity Map

Porter, noted Harvard Business School professor and renowned strategy guru, said it best: "Successful companies *cannot* delight and retain every single customer." It's true that a winning strategy "deliberately makes some customers unhappy."

We had a retail client who hated coupons, loyalty discounts, and the like. He cringed at the thought of two different customers paying different prices for the same goods. What would the customer who paid more think if she found out? He couldn't stand the thought of alienating her. But if you think about it, how can you possibly implement CRM without a differentiated experience? By definition, you can't do it if every customer and prospect experiences the same thing.

Harrah's was one of the first companies to intimately study its customers and openly show preferential treatment toward its most valuable guests—complimentary drinks, room upgrades, prime rib dinners, and so forth. As an infrequent guest of the company's hotels and casinos, if you want the same special treatment, then your goal is to become more like those preferred customers. You want to know why they receive perks and incentives that you don't receive. You aspire to meet the criteria of value and loyalty that will take you to the next level of appreciation. So no, differentiated experiences aren't going to make every customer happy. And this should be by design. Marketers need to ask themselves: Do I have the stomach for it? How will I handle the phone calls from those disgruntled customers? Am I prepared to either help them grow or let them go?

THE HEART OF THE MATTER

Following are some of the key ideas to think about from this chapter as you implement customer strategy as a business strategy in your organization:

- Allowing multiple silos within the organization to establish their own customer strategies leads to inconsistent customer treatment from touchpoint to touchpoint. These varying treatments become the potholes that prevent a smooth path to cCRM value. *Enterprise-wide* means that customer strategy is established from the top down and permeates all functions: customer facing and noncustomer facing.
- There must be a mutually beneficial relationship between the company and the customer, and the company must define and cultivate that relationship better than competitors. This requires several factors at the root of customer strategy: customer portfolio management, segmentation, and segment strategy.
- *Customer portfolio management* refers to optimization of financial metrics across the entire portfolio of customers. Segmentation breaks the portfolio into manageable pieces

that the organization can rally around. *Segmentation strategy* encompasses the final complementary components enabling an organization to act in a unified manner, making coherent investment decisions and delivering a consistent and yet differentiated experience.

- Not all companies need to be operating at level 5 on the cCRM maturity continuum. The goal is to achieve optimization at the lowest possible level of maturity to retain competitive advantage.

Chapter 6 Experience Delivery

Finding the Sweet Spot for Expert Customer Integration

If you don't believe that data-driven experiences are going to continue to evolve and explode, becoming a crucial component of a customer-centric business strategy, just take a look at Google Glass. It'll soon be clear that customer experience is no longer just about media and channels. It's going to be all around us, literally, in front of our eyes at every waking moment. Our lives—as marketers and consumers—are going to be all about data-driven experiences.

We in the marketing profession are accustomed to building arsenals. We develop all these tool sets, bring them to scale, and then try to launch them toward customers. We've been doing this for years, but I propose that we rethink our approach. Instead of starting with the arsenal of products and then retrofitting the customer experience, we need to first think about what the customer data-driven experiences actually need to be, and then start to build solid tool sets that will enable those experiences. The company's placement on the customer relationship marketing (CRM) maturity continuum is a key consideration here. In levels 1 to 3, marketers don't have the expertise or tools to drive experience in today's highly complex, tech-driven world. They know brands and targeting, but they need to know how to drive the *experience* in a seamless, integrated way.

As we refer to customer experience, we are talking about the creation of connected programs that drive desired customer behaviors. Those experiences can be one-offs, in the form of triggered encounters based on specific behaviors by the customer, such as a 10 percent discount offer when a customer starts to abandon a shopping cart. Or they could be a series of interactions where you're guiding the customer to the point that you want them to go. Picture the consumer who receives a direct mail piece, executes a search, views a display ad, follows a personalized URL (PURL) to a customized Web page, doesn't complete a transaction, is retargeted with display, returns to the site, and executes a transaction. The latter starts to build what I call moments of truth across different channels and media, where data is brought to the customer experience. Each interaction is informed by the prior interactions. And ultimately, of course, to enable these moments of truth, you must have the infrastructure, data, and analytics as core enablers, and the customer strategy design and financial management tools must be in place to inform decisions about the right mix of budget dollars to the individual touchpoints.

So in the context of Connected CRM (cCRM), where does customer experience fit in? It begins with ideation—the creation of what that customer value proposition is going to be and how it will be conveyed across touchpoints. This includes what the offer is going to be, what the message is going to be, what the creative is going to be, and how it's going to be delivered.

Customer experience is important because it's where the rubber meets the road. This is it, where the customer interacts with the brand; this is what the customer sees. We could have the most advanced analytics possible, as strong an infrastructure as we want, and a tremendous amount of creative capability, but unless we're able to actually deliver in that moment of truth, who cares?

That's where an established cCRM program management structure becomes crucial. It encompasses a strategy and a program blueprint built toward the end state: setting the foundation for the behavior we want to drive. Then comes experience design: the interactions, the offers, the messages, and the creative. It's all about how the customer experiences it. And finally, there's the execution side of it. What media will be used to deliver outbound messages? What channels will support them? Whom are we targeting and by what means? How am I personalizing within the customer segments, and to what level of customization?

FINDING THE SWEET SPOT

It's likely you've seen one of those extreme playgrounds—the big ones that are three stories high, with a series of brightly colored tunnels, nets, and slides and twisting mesh walkways that feed into bubble-shaped containers, linking to slides that spit kids out somewhere on the other side of the park. Basically, it's a life-sized hamster "habitrail" for children. Kids love it. Parents loathe it.

As a parent, going there for the first time can be quite nerve-racking. Your instinct is to follow your kid through the maze of tunnels and slides. These tunnels aren't designed to fit most adults, so you find yourself squeezing through the meshed infrastructure, clinging to the shirttail of your child, desperately trying to keep up with the scramble toward another slide leading to who knows where.

During a short break, while your child sits and watches a bug crawl on a leaf, you take a moment to look around. You notice that right in the middle of all this mayhem, two mothers are sitting perfectly still while everyone else in the place is just nuts. Other parents are trying to leave, desperately pushing lunch on their kids or pleading, "Let's go get ice cream, honey." But amidst all this chaos, these two mothers have found a way to remain calm, peaceful, and relaxed—free to call a friend, read a magazine, or simply enjoy watching their children play.

Eagerly, you venture over to those Zen-like mothers to see what's going on. How can they be so relaxed? What makes them so special? Sitting down next to them you find your answer. From their "special place," their vantage point, you can see all the exits, every tunnel, slide, walkway, and rope ladder. Just sitting still as the disorder swirls around you everywhere, you are able to see your child, and with minimal effort.

But remaining still isn't easy. You are compelled to go follow your kid. Even knowing what you now know, it's hard to shake your old ways. Your instinct is to chase.

Developing successful marketing programs can elicit similar emotions.

It often feels like a scramble. In many ways, our customers are a lot like kids at the playground. They are constantly distracted, always running, grabbing for the next shiny object, tech device, or interesting link, anything to quench their informational thirst. As marketers, we spend too much of our time chasing them through tunnels, scampering up nets to get their attention just long enough to entice them to have ice cream with us.

What can we learn from the Zen mothers and their sweet spot when thinking about building marketing programs for our customers?

Approaching program development using the framework of cCRM to construct how we communicate with our audience will allow us to see the blind spots and spend less time, energy, and resources. But first we must squash our instinct to scramble and change our approach to reaching our customers.

BRIDGING CUSTOMER STRATEGY TO PROGRAM DESIGN

Before laying brick to any program construction, we first take clear direction from the insights of our earlier customer strategy efforts (Figure 6.1). We now know much more about our

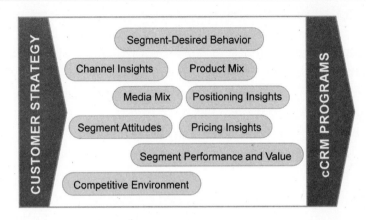

FIGURE 6.1   Bridging Customer Insights

audiences through our segmentation plan. We know how these audiences behave, how they perceive our value proposition, what their channel habits are, and even what their pricing perspectives are. We have a good understanding of the kinds of products and offerings our customers gravitate toward. We also know what they are already seeing from the competition and where we are winning or losing.

All of this segment-driven information drives how we develop our programs and how we think about our programs in terms of accommodating the differences in our audiences. We've seen this recently with a sports apparel provider who sought to understand the differences in purchase decisions among its customer segments. Understanding how audiences make choices is crucial to building effective programs. In one group, we found that selecting sports clothing is something that fulfills their inner desire to fit in socially—a decidedly image-conscious position. Another group was focused on the performance of their outerwear—a technology-driven approach. For these high-tech individuals, the choice was about what will make them both faster and more comfortable. Digging in further we realized that these differences in buying habits would require us to communicate with these customers in dramatically different ways, so much so that separate programs or campaigns would be needed to connect meaningfully with both groups. Exposing these contrasting purchasing inclinations early on is one way we can bridge the divide between our customer strategy and the needs of our marketing programs.

CONNECTED PROGRAMS

Connected programs are developed by first understanding how they will influence or support the customer's life cycle. This forms the basis for our program design by combining deep customer insight with what is necessary to motivate a customer from one stage to the next (Figure 6.2).

Remember those performance junkies from our sports apparel example? Moving them from the first purchase to second purchase is important for them to enter the loyalty stage in the life cycle. What will it take for us to reach them specifically to trigger

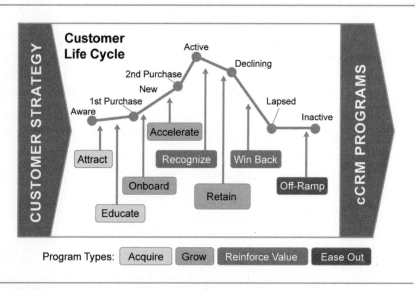

FIGURE 6.2   Influencing Customer Life Cycle

another buying situation? The onboarding program must contain all the elements needed to motivate the customer's unique buying habits. Pulling from early insights will inform timing and primary messages and will even offer specifics. We may need to provide a new communication or program activity to influence this segment at this moment in their life cycle. It's possible our offer will require a landing page experience showcasing the product technology—reminding customers that our brand fulfills their desire for the highest-performing apparel. Additionally, the product category will be a key influencer, and analyzing customers' first purchase specifics will drive the exact messaging and product suggestions needed for a successful second purchase.

We know that the activities of an onboarding program are vastly different from, say, a win-back initiative, yet what is required to influence a segment's behavior may be very similar. Both programs are attempting to keep a customer by moving that person from a state of inactivity to loyalty. Aiming to get that second purchase from a new customer during onboarding can be no different from the one purchase needed to win back a loyal customer.

Connected programs don't exist in isolation. Multiple programs often must work together to effectively support those customer life cycles. cCRM enables us, through its infrastructure, to more easily combine programs so that they can learn from each other and deliver better results. Because it is now possible through our segment-driven analytics to track how we've interacted with a customer in the past, we can inform what we need to do for them during a future program activity. This is a core requirement for advancement to the fifth level of CRM maturity. Anything that customers were most drawn to during an awareness program can be applied later toward an acceleration program. For example, maybe a customer began his journey using an online financial planning tool for a retirement program. How did he first interact with the tool? Which of our financial content did he initially gravitate toward? What other financial products were browsed? Using what we know about how this customer was first attracted to us can help when trying to retain him later. Which of our financial products or offers might influence him during a declining phase in his life cycle? Can we position our retention content and offer details around a topic such as retirement, which we already know is important to the customer?

Our programs must learn from each other. All of the customer actions occurring in other programs can be considered in cCRM. Identifying those actions that cross multiple programs for the same individual will enable us to customize our messaging and offers within a program. It is therefore paramount that we construct our programs knowing that this knowledge-share must occur.

PROGRAM DEVELOPMENT

Using what we know about the segment attitudes and preferences, the marketable universe, and desired customer behaviors we can assemble the best set of customer activities into a data-informed CRM program.

The program architecture must have a segmented focus. By addressing the desired marketing behavior within the lens of the segment, we can pinpoint how our program needs to be available to our various audiences.

Everything within our program must roll into what is known about the segments. Messages, offers, and creative content are all derived from what will resonate with each audience type.

When organizing a program, we should ask ourselves: How do we align our messaging approach, our inventory of offers, and the things that we can do from a business point of view, including the creative treatment itself, to each audience (Figure 6.3)? What messages should we create to accommodate the differences between our audiences? What could we curate from other sources to allow for even more content variation? What are some things we already have available within our organization, online or offline, that could be repurposed for this program?

SEGMENT-DESIRED BEHAVIOR		
Messages Develop relevant and personalized messaging based on segment or individual and behavior	**Offers** Determine relevancy of offer (and offer rotation) for each distinct segment	**Treatment** Establish creative rotation and versions within segments and behaviors

PERSONALIZATION ENABLERS Inventory opportunities for customization	
Right Media Select most applicable media for each of the audience segments	**Right Channel** Select optimal response channels to achieve program strategy objectives

FIGURE 6.3   cCRM Program Architecture

An inventory of all personalization enablers is also required. Because every moment can be customized, we need to spend some time thinking about what can positively influence our customers' behaviors, whether it's purchase history or the frequency with which they are viewing certain content on your e-commerce site. What is a driver of their behavior? What is something that we can act upon? Ultimately, we want to know how they are currently participating with us. What are the right media to use? What are the right channels? Our segmentation effort has already exposed some of this insight, but program design can often uncover new possibilities.

Personalization isn't just about being relevant. In many cases it can be used to lower the hurdle to conversion. Filling out online applications is a big stumbling block for most companies. It's often perceived as too much work and will turn away many otherwise interested customers. Because marketers already have access to many pieces of customer information, we can alter a cumbersome application process by turning off nonessential elements. Rather than burdening the customer with a sea of input boxes, in most cases we can now reduce these application forms by half. Decreasing the customer effort has resulted in remarkable increases in the number of completed applications. The business still gets its necessary information without creating extra hassle for the customer.

But remember, although personalization is a key component of customer-focused communications, customization is where the money is. Recognizing me as a person has value, but customizing my brand experience has so much more. It's one thing to say, "Thank you for flying United Airlines, Mr. Williams," but handing me a boarding pass that automatically reflects an upgraded first-class seat is quite another.

PROGRAM BLUEPRINTS

Typically, more than one team is building a program. Communication across efforts is important to ensure the flexibility and connectedness we are aiming toward. A visual tool is helpful for keeping seamless understanding across a marketing environment. Stakeholders need to stay abreast of various programs without being burdened with the details.

Program blueprints are a great communication instrument for driving interest and support within a marketing organization. These blueprints define the individual components of each program to align the client and cross-functional team around the goals, expected results, and the test-learn agenda for each program. Most brands we work with have teams consisting of many different business owners. From merchandising, website, and internal analytics leaders to product designers, financial advisors, and sales leaders, we must learn to speak to all interested parties collectively by finding a common language. The website leader may be focused on acquisition and conversion, whereas the merchandiser is concerned with how often the current hot product can be mentioned in the market. Another imperative is forming a plan for customer communication governance—a crucial step for moving a CRM capability up to levels 4 and 5 in the maturity continuum. And the first step for governance is getting owner alignment on the objectives of the program, well before the details are chased. This saves dollars and time, not to mention avoiding all the headaches that come from lack of clarity. Our program blueprints can help this kind of alignment by speaking to several priorities at once (Figure 6.4).

High-Value Cross Sell

PROGRAM SUMMARY

1. Modify existing registration/purchase confirmation to welcome stream.

2. Drive traffic, provide orientation, and capture additional content information.

3. Assumptions: EM is deploying to whole audience segment, and DM is only a subset (those showing interest). Messaging will differ depending on origination of contact.

SEGMENT SPECIFICS

 34% share | Lead index 90% | Conversion 125% | Lapse rate 8%
Price sensitive, image conscious, early tech adopter, heavy mobile usage

DESIRED BEHAVIOR

Drive registration, customer preferences, and additional sales.

KEY MARKETING TACTICS

Dynamic EM X-sell components, personalized display retargeting, behavioral triggers EM/DM

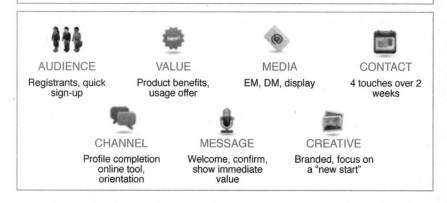

FIGURE 6.4   Program Blueprint: Simplified

This blueprint will typically communicate things such as program objectives, segment highlights, our desired customer behavior, and key marketing tactics. For example, our program might require a new dynamic e-mail that contains cross-sell components. Multiple teams in the organization may have to work in tandem to provide the content and measurement for this to be successful.

The blueprint can be a guide for making decisions across multiple programs. For example, a complex, versioned landing page might be suggested for two different programs. By including details such as profit drivers, audience value, or channel usage details, the stakeholders can get a better idea of which program might deserve the extra expense.

Ultimately, the blueprint communicates directly to the next phase of development, what we call experience design. Once stakeholder agreement has taken place for our programs, we can begin designing the best experiences needed to drive our desired customer behaviors.

CONNECTED EXPERIENCE DESIGN

A connected experience learns from the group to provide for the individual. Segment behavior constantly influences how we craft and adjust our thinking. How do we know what is best for the individual? First observe the audience in which that person belongs. When we determine what is working for the segment, we can better customize for the individual.

A connected experience enables personalization at the interaction layer, influences the customer journey progression, and provides customer life cycle support.

- Personalization efforts consider what can be customized to have the highest impact for customer response. How can we make every touch as relevant and meaningful as possible for our customers?

- The journey progression determines the most effective ways to move a customer through the stages of a customer journey. How will we influence a customer in their progress within our experience?
- Life cycle planning defines the best engagement over the long term with the customer. What are the best ways for all of our touchpoints to inform that longer relationship?

Experience design also focuses on the touchpoints or customer interactions, be it clicking a link in an e-mail, viewing a video, reading a mobile notification, conversing with a call center representative, visiting a store, checking into a hotel, or eating at a restaurant.

Interactions are the lifeblood of a connected program. Our interactions always have a focused message, an appropriate offer, and a creative expression that is relevant for the customer. When planning for interactions we focus on questions such as: What are the most relevant offers for the audience at this stage in the journey? How does this interaction's message need to change depending on the segment being engaged? What's the best emphasis of creative at this moment?

To answer these questions, we can use insights gained from ongoing program analytics, the performance of past programs, or the performance of the current program (Figure 6.5). All the

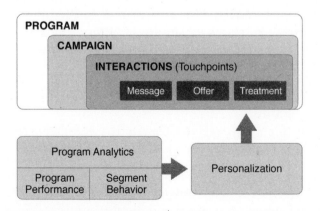

FIGURE 6.5   Interaction Elements

things that we know about the segment are going to inform how we can personalize each interaction. Working recently with a major video game publisher on a sports title that is updated based on real-world league performance, we experienced first-hand the needs of a connected program and the speed with which communications must relate to the evolving game play. Typically, marketing would influence only the launch of such a video game, but with a cCRM program, marketing communications can be coordinated with ongoing game events. We can continue to involve customers well after purchase—triggering personal messages relating to the activities they care about the most and identifying special cross-selling opportunities, such as suggesting upcoming game titles that relate to the kinds of game play users participate with the most. Conversely, through cCRM, publishers can learn how to announce and target new game events to drive even more participation among loyal customers, thus taking the video game experience well beyond the console and tapping into the passions of the customer for future purchases.

INTERACTION PATHWAYS

Customer interactions, of course, rarely occur in isolation. Customers are often performing actions that link directly to other actions. A series of multiple interactions that move a customer from one journey stage to the next are what we call an interaction pathway. It considers what customer action is required and which media and channels are necessary to support those interactions.

Plotting out these various user paths is helpful for showing potential problem areas and highlighting opportunities (Figure 6.6). We may expose an unnecessary step, a confusing bottleneck, or an opportunity for a new creative approach.

Knowing where a customer is likely to have originated can help us design a better interaction. For example, let's say a

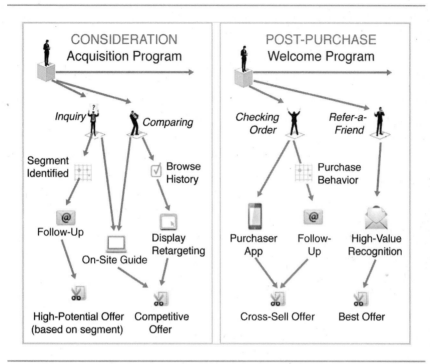

FIGURE 6.6   Interaction Pathways: Simplified

customer is in the process of comparing products. Whether choosing among various product attributes, brand promises, or price points, we may drive that person to an on-site guide to enable easier decision making. When we then trigger a competitive offer through a retargeting effort, we'll need to understand what customer action occurred in order to craft the best message for our offer. How was the customer making decisions? Do we know the product categories the customer saw? Can we predict which product types will be in that person's consideration set based on the segment in which he or she belongs? We may not always have control over these paths, but when making interaction design decisions, it's helpful to know where a customer came from or where the customer is going.

MESSAGE ARCHITECTURE

The majority of messaging strategies originate from the brand promise. It is often the leading thought that customers are familiar with regarding a company and its offering, although in recent years this is changing with more customers touching a brand within a direct channel before any mass media exposure. Product positioning usually follows the brand promise in a messaging hierarchy. We are asking, What's the promise of the product, and what might that mean for our audience? Together the brand and the product promises are expressed for mass media delivery (Figure 6.7).

However, for CRM or direct marketing, we require an additional kind of promise: a focused promise. Our targeted audiences often need directed language for what we are communicating. Of course, we need to derive our messaging approach from both the brand promise and the product promise, but we also need a focused way of saying it. Take, for example, Philips' "Sense and Simplicity" as a brand promise. Philips

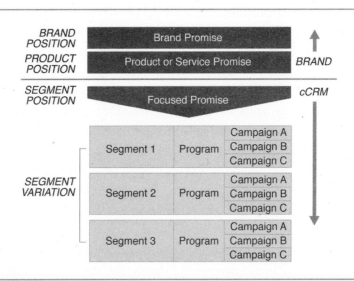

FIGURE 6.7   cCRM Message Architecture

promises the idea of better home living through the products it sells. Life is better when one's senses are comforted with simple technology. When that promise moves into more specific customer communication, the message needs to be directed toward something that relates to what we know about the segment or individual. An example could be addressing a customer who has bought a Philips product in the past and now is interested in energy-saving lighting. The message might transform from the broad "sense and simplicity" to the focused "Enjoy what you'd expect from a Philips product: quality light (senses), while spending less on energy (simplicity)." This directed language, reflective of the attitudes of the segment or individual, is more meaningful and motivational to the customer.

MESSAGE-OFFER-CREATIVE SEQUENCING

The order of what we say is just as important as our focused messages. Driven by analytics, we can inform our marketing interactions beyond just the first touch to allow for more relevant messaging for customer interactions over time. There are many reasons to sequence a message: to avoid being repetitive, to capitalize on a specific customer action, or to emphasize a different part of an offer.

Figure 6.8 shows how our first two messages are very segment-driven. They have to be because we know little about the individual at this point. We lead with the offer, what is known to be enticing to this segment. Moving on to the second message, we now know what they've already seen (and ignored), so supplying it again would be wasteful. This time we will lead with a benefit highlight or something very specific about the product that may resonate with our segment.

Things get interesting once we identify a customer, which may be done through participation, cookie tracking, or user authentication. We now can do much more to customize our messages. Our third message mentions the offer once again, but this time

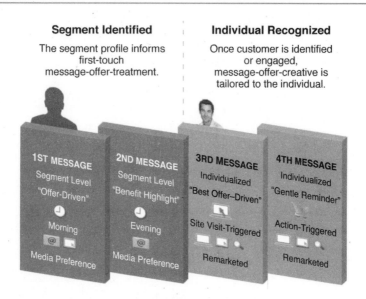

FIGURE 6.8   Message Sequencing

we can change the details of the offer. Let's say this individual sits in a higher customer value chain in our segment. Increasing the offer value could be a way for us to demonstrate better customer recognition, thus improving our response rate with this person in the future. We could also factor in a recent behavior (such as a site visit, browsing habits, past purchase), which will influence how we can motivate the customer through our offer delivery. All of this will bring us that much closer to our customer. We can make the experience that much richer and more meaningful.

MESSAGE-OFFER LOGIC (MESSAGING DECISION TREE)

Determining how the experience changes based on customer action helps us understand how we can be both consistent and effective with our communication to the customer.

Figure 6.9 is a much more simplified version of what we typically would need to do, but it is helpful to create a visual map

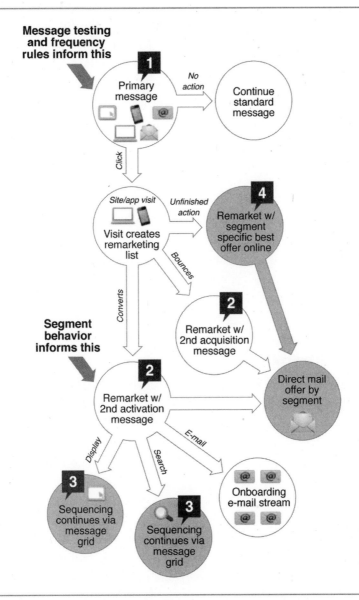

FIGURE 6.9   Messaging Decision Tree: Simplified

for all the different customer actions that trigger subsequent messages. Using our interaction pathways as a guide we can determine the best messages for each occasion.

Message testing, frequency rules, and ongoing segment performance will also continue to inform this logic. If during the first time we ran this sequence our segments didn't really react as well as we had hoped, we can learn from the group and make changes to help our messages resonate next time. A detailed understanding of message logic can help us creatively build out our experiences.

CONNECTED CREATIVE

When we think about creating interactions for connected experiences, we think about it a bit differently than a brand campaign. At the brand level, things need to be large, universally appealing, and, as such, they are often generalized. Much of what we create for direct response is going to be individualized. Those expressions need to be flexible for easy relevance across various audience types. They need to really hit home with the segment.

Building a connected experience must start with what can be personal—experiences that can be directed toward an individual's view of the brand. Rather than starting with the needs of a mass audience and trying to please a large and typically unknown group, we begin with what will most resonate with the individual.

Connected creative begins with insight into the audience, focuses on the preferences and underlying motivations of the segment, and aims to fulfill the brand promise at every customer interaction. Our inspiration always comes from what can be micropersonalized for the needs of our customers.

This customer-centered approach ushers in an evolution of the creative contribution to the marketing realm, including how agencies—and their clients, for that matter—build, develop, and sustain great brands. Brand policies are replaced by brand principles, as appropriateness is measured less by strict adherence to lengthy brand standards manuals and more by conformity to a core set of universal brand truths and promises. Brand managers must become brand coaches. They must spend more time helping empower their organizations and agencies to optimize the memorability and shareability of specific marketing moments and less time enforcing static brand laws in every nook and cranny of the marketing landscape. Monolithic brand identity systems develop into a holistic brand ecosystem, where compelling individual experiences enliven and expand the brand—and where clients and agencies will find the most tangible, most profitable contributions to the living, ongoing learning relationship between brands and individuals.

PROGRAM EXECUTION AND MANAGEMENT

Once we've established what our customer experiences are going to be, the task becomes how to deliver them with optimal results. For clarity, I consider media to be the vehicles of outbound communication and channel to be the place where consumers come to interact with the brand. Often the vehicles overlap, but generally, that's my rule of thumb. For example, the channel would be the website, and the media would be display advertising that drives you there. Building out that media and that channel experience is a tremendous undertaking. In fact, I'd argue this portion of the cCRM framework probably represents the largest amount of activity. Executing campaigns across multiple media and developing channel assets to support them requires a significant effort.

In the previous chapter, we discussed the customer strategy component of the cCRM framework and the segment brief that comes out of that function. Using the segment brief to inform the experience delivery function, a program plan is conceived to drive specific behaviors within the designated segments. The next phase of the experience delivery component is to develop a media plan and a channel plan that will support it. Specifically, on the media side, we're talking about addressable media. We want to be able to start targeting at the segment level and ultimately move to the individual level.

From a media perspective, you must have a multi-dimensional strategy that encompasses targeting, personalization, campaign management, and then, obviously, ongoing optimization. On the channel side, it's more about development, implementation, personalization, and ultimately continuous optimization.

This dovetails with the infrastructure conversation that I'll cover in Chapter 8, which speaks to the technology enablement tools that use data and analytics to create customized moments in the chosen media and channels. The infrastructure enables the ongoing measurement and reporting capabilities to support the segment and individual behavior metrics.

When we talk about tactics, we can easily get bogged down in the silos of digital and offline touchpoints. Take addressable media. I don't think that there are a lot of universal addressable media plans today. There are separate discussions around the direct mail plan, the display targeting plan, and potentially the addressable television plan, but we're typically looking at those plans separately. We believe we need to start to look at them holistically.

So, even though targeting strategies for the various media and channels are unique within each tactic, it is important to also take a holistic view with a comprehensive addressable media plan, because interactions must be connected across a program. This means there must be a common segmentation scheme, a similar message theme by segment. But within the context of that plan, not only do we have to select the different media we're going to use, but we have to use different targeting styles within each.

For example, you could be targeting in display while doing an audience match on Facebook. In search, you could be doing value-based bidding on individual keywords that are tied to a segment level. In mobile, you could be doing push notification or short message service (SMS) to show the next best offer. Or in display, you could take somebody who came to your site and looked at a few products and retarget that person for the next two weeks in alternate media with that same product set, in case that person is still in the market.

Within each medium, you have to be thinking about what each different tactic is going to be and then personalize where you can. When no personalization opportunity exists, you drive to the segment level. The campaign management around this is significant and often requires a number of different tool sets. No one integrated campaign management platform is available for all addressable media. You might have to use an ExactTarget, for example, as your e-mail deployment engine, whereas in display advertising, you might need to use a demand side platform (DSP), such as MediaMath; in mobile, a mobile push SMS platform such as Waterfall; or for direct mail, a direct mail campaign management software such as Unica.

It takes many different tool sets to execute these addressable media campaigns. And on the channel execution side, delivering segment-based or personalized communications is a similar story, whether you're building websites that can enable offers and creative experiences, building Facebook apps, or educating salespeople at the point of sale. One of Merkle's major insurance clients is in the throes of implementing enterprise segmentation, which involves a tremendous amount of work in their call centers to embrace the segmentation. This includes extensive training as well as scripting by segment.

Think of an insurance company expanding into mobile. Today, not only can customers shop and purchase insurance online, they can speed through the claims process, right from the scene of the accident. That's a game-changing type of customer experience. If you think back to the discussion in Chapter 2 about the spectrum between being campaign focused and customer focused, this kind of move breaks right through the glass ceiling. Where personalization of e-mails might be a level 2 tactic, this move says, "We're taking the company straight to level 5."

With the advent of responsive design, Web channels can be formatted to instantly render based on the type of device being used. With consumers engaging through multiple different devices that have varying screen sizes and functionality, responsive design is a way to keep the experience consistent. Progressive brands from Safeway to Victoria's Secret to L.L.Bean are already using these capabilities and revolutionizing customer experience across devices.

Social media is another groundbreaking customer experience opportunity. And it's not just about listening and keywords. Facebook's open graph solution allows marketers to create customer experiences based on Facebook user data at the site domain. Hearst Magazines is using Facebook's open graph today to capture social data in an exchange of value with its customers, right at the site.

Experience delivery is a crucial component to a cCRM approach. And the bottom line is that marketing programs must integrate media and channels to drive these experiences. It can't be done one at a time in silos. You must start with segment-based experiences but ultimately work toward providing individual-level experiences. We now have the data, the technology, and the ability to drive it there. Remember that this is about designing, building, and running customer experiences. Being good at one of these is simply not good enough. You have to be strong at all three.

THE HEART OF THE MATTER

As you develop your customer experience strategies in your organization, following are some of the main points to remember from this chapter:

- cCRM programs must bridge many gaps that can derail a cCRM strategy: differences in customer behavior by segment, variances in product offerings, and even disparate customer objectives, such as acquisition, growth, win-back, loyalty, and so on. Therefore, program architecture must have a multi-dimensional approach with a focus on segmentation.

- Because it's not feasible to create a unique personal message for every individual customer, we must design customer experiences with an eye toward personalization, which begins at the segment level. Program analytics can answer ongoing questions about customer preferences, life stage, offer strength, message effectiveness, and so on. These insights inform how we personalize each interaction.

- Although targeting strategies and tactics differ within each form of media and channel, programs must create interactions that connect across them all: mobile SMS, targeted display, search, social, e-mail, postal mail, and everything in between. Marketing programs must consider how media and channels can be planned and designed in combination to drive effective experiences.

Chapter 7 Financial Management

You Can't Optimize What You Can't Measure

I can't stress enough the importance of measurement in Connected Customer Relationship Marketing (cCRM). You simply cannot, even under the best of circumstances, do without it. The fundamental question, whose answer continues to be elusive to marketers, is "What value do marketing and sales efforts drive within our business?" The question is so simple, its importance so obvious, and the challenge so overwhelming. The proliferation of data, the advancement in computing power, the increasing focus on analytics, and the sea of metrics we study every day somehow have not translated into significant progress toward fixing our measurement problem.

The fragmentation of touchpoints, brought about in large part by the digital revolution, presents distinct challenges for the marketer. With the ever-growing number of media and channels at our disposal, measurement is complex at best. Consumers are exposed to a plethora of competing messages from offline and online media. Further complicating matters, they are reaching out to brands through an equally staggering number of channels.

In fact, the days when an organization defined its brand and pushed it to consumers is over. Consumers have just as much control over what your brand represents as you do. This is not to say that creating a brand or mass media vehicles is no longer important. In fact, when you consider how much influence friends, online reviews, and social networks have on a buying decision, it has become even more important to manage what your brand represents. It is *how* an organization manages its brand that is changing.

It is tempting to think about measurement sophistication as a back office operation, with mathematicians debating esoteric formulas, rather than something of strategic importance deserving C-level attention. But consider a fundamental idiom that presumably everyone would subscribe to: "Do more of what performs well and less of what performs poorly." This approach works only when an accurate measurement platform is in place. If we can't accurately measure performance, why would we assume our targeting or budget allocation decisions are improving performance? You can't optimize what you can't measure, and if you don't have a reliable measurement platform, you are throwing darts all over the place.

In fact, the situation is often even worse than just picking random numbers. It's not that marketers don't have metrics to base decisions on; in fact, most marketers are swimming in them. The problem is that the metrics being used are not measuring what they say they are measuring. This can result in our being misled into thinking we must improve a metric that may not even be driving business value. Not only are we throwing darts at the wall all around the target, we aren't even aiming at the right target to begin with.

Consider GEICO's evolution during the first decade of this century. Over that time period the success of its direct marketing program drove an increase in its direct mail volume of more than 600 percent. A primary measurement approach was to use something called indirect attribution. Essentially, when someone received a quote for auto insurance, we looked back to see if that person received a mail piece within the three weeks leading up to the quote process. If so, we attributed that quote to the mail piece. Around 2010, GEICO was targeting as much as 90 percent of households in limited geographies with an average of 12 mail pieces per year per household, or one per month. Given a three-week response window, with some people receiving a mail piece every four weeks, this means that about two-thirds of people in these geographies who responded would have received a mail piece within the response window, meaning about two-thirds of all quotes in these geographies would be attributed to direct mail. Because GEICO spends significantly less than that percentage of its marketing budget on direct mail, an analysis of the return on investment (ROI) of different media would reveal that direct mail is by far the most effective medium, leading to the conclusion to move more money out of other media (low relative performance) and into direct mail (high performing media), right? Wrong. Conversely, an added challenge associated with this measurement approach is that you might be targeting people who would ask for a quote anyway.

Another example of how incorrect measurement leads to detrimental budget allocation is digital display retargeting. The context is simple: A consumer visits your website, researches your product, and ultimately leaves without making a purchase. Afterward, we serve a digital display ad to that same consumer when the opportunity arises through real-time bidding platforms. Measurement is done through last-click attribution, so this retargeting program appears to perform well above any other digital display platform. The problem once again is a matter of incremental performance. How many of those consumers will end up buying your product anyway? The retargeting online display ad may not be driving the outcome; you just happen to be able to target them while they are in the buying process. Plus, when multiple display programs are happening simultaneously (which is often the case), measurements for all of those programs will show that retargeting creates the highest click-through rate. Now we get into a situation where that consumer is targeted more than 20 times a day. Finally, this misled targeting will choke off the sales funnel, by focusing marketing efforts on retargeting rather than bringing in new potential customers.

When you consider the cCRM maturity model, it is evident that financial management as a capability is prevalent across all five levels. Every organization makes budget allocation decisions based on information from past programs. The question is not whether you are doing it, but rather how effectively are you doing it. There is a significant financial management characteristic that dictates movement from level 3 to level 4 in the maturity model: the integrated measurement platform. An integrated measurement platform implies that you have cross-media measurement processes and algorithms in place and that the data required to enable this measurement is continually loaded into a data and technology infrastructure to enable an ongoing measurement system. The establishment of this measurement platform is one of the key challenges that makes moving from level 3 to level 4 so difficult.

All media are trending toward individual-level targeting in real time. As this happens, marketers have the opportunity to take advantage of the ever-increasing ways to communicate with potential buyers. They can be more targeted than ever before, and they can quickly shift marketing budgets very quickly. A tremendous opportunity to gain a competitive advantage exists for those marketers who can accurately and quickly understand what is working and what isn't working and then shift future marketing spend to optimize performance. Of course, the flipside is also true. Marketers who can't take advantage will be left behind by those who can. Or even worse, they will be misled by faulty performance metrics and end up not even shooting at the correct target.

Even though the opportunity to target at an individual level is here, we can't create media plans at an individual level, and with rare exceptions, we can't develop products for each individual. In addition, we can't create different television spots for each individual. Because of that, segmentation still plays a critical role in measurement and planning decisions. Marketers need to embrace segment-level media planning (many already are). Segments can be based on attitudes, values, or life stage. The key is to enable the measurement, forecasting, and media mix optimization to occur by segment. The financial management section of the cCRM framework deals with measurement and decision making at a segment level. In others words, the focus is more macro level as to how organizations best use their marketing budgets to drive optimal ROIs.

In the cCRM framework we define *financial management* as how we consistently measure the value of consumer interactions with the brand and how that information is used to make future marketing decisions. Measurement is an enterprise-wide currency.

When considering the breadth of this definition, it becomes clear that developing a world-class financial management competency is far more than just implementing a new piece of software or hiring a couple of statisticians. Rather, the implications of broad redefinition of metrics and how they are calculated can affect all areas of the organization, including existing processes and compensation plans. Therefore, it is critical not only to get all the nuts and bolts right but also to properly manage the cultural change to ensure adoption across groups and at all levels. Because of the broad reaching nature it is essential to have alignment from the chief marketing officer (CMO) and potentially chief financial officer (CFO).

The financial management framework shown in Figure 7.1 has proved to be an effective way to conceptualize the financial management area of the cCRM framework.

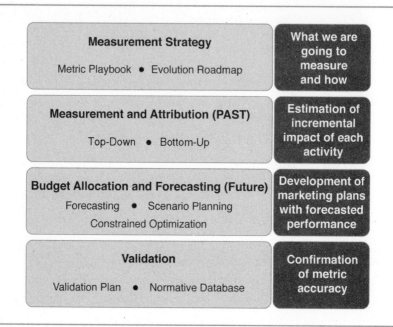

FIGURE 7.1 Financial Management Framework

MEASUREMENT STRATEGY

Measurement strategy is a framework used to ensure an organization properly scopes and plans to implement a world-class financial management system. In our opinion, you don't have a measurement strategy unless it covers the following five areas.

1. *A measurement strategy must have complete metrics.* In other words, nothing is out of scope. A great example of this is an organization that spends a significant amount of money on broad media, such as TV. Often TV is used as a broad media designed to drive a softer metric such as awareness or perception. It therefore is common to have a situation where direct and digital media are measured on an ROI basis but TV is left out because it was designed to drive a different outcome. Not having complete metrics makes the measurement framework break down. How can we arbitrate

between spending more on TV or more on digital media? The metrics are not analogous and therefore like comparing apples and oranges. The solution is likely not to try to force TV to be measured on the same metric as direct and digital media, but rather to expand the measurement framework to include awareness or perception metrics. Next, ensure research studies are designed in a way that enables identification of significant shifts in awareness or perception. Then assign an ROI (or whatever common metric being used) to changes in that metric. This ensures that nothing is left out of the framework and also enables cross-functional adoption, since the change in metric is not being forced.

2. *Within a measurement strategy, metrics must be applied consistently.* We regularly see organizations with a metric such as cost per acquisition (CPA), which they compare across programs. For example, digital display, paid search, and direct mail can all generate a CPA metric. Assume direct mail is measured using a test control design and therefore creating a true incremental CPA metric. But then assume search and display are calculated using direct attribution methods. It's likely that search and display will generate better CPA estimates than direct mail simply because they are calculated using different methods. Calculating a metric such as CPA in a consistent manner to represent the same thing across media and programs is essential to a measurement strategy.

3. *The metrics need to be applicable across all measurement levels.* Marketing mix models are very effective at creating a single metric across all media, but this method can't estimate the same metric at a very granular level within media. Often, organizations use other metrics at a granular level, such as cost per click or cost per response. The challenge is that at a quarterly or yearly planning level, metrics from the media mix are used to establish budgets and goals, but then each media owner can't calculate those same metrics day to day at the level of granularity by which the planning decisions were made. This is why it is essential that the metrics can be generated at all measurement levels.

4. *The metrics have to be applicable across all measurement dimensions. Dimensions* in this context refers to common ways by which an organization would likely want to break out a metric. Geography and time are common dimensions. Organizations want to know what the cost per sale is by month or by state, for example. Another common and powerful dimension is customer segment. What is the cost per sale by segment? It is important to plan early on how metrics will be sliced by these dimensions. If we care about a metric such as brand awareness, for example, we may need to increase sample size and ask specific questions to be able to report on brand awareness by segment.

5. *The right method must be used for each metric.* This is critical. There is no measurement method that is the best choice in every instance. Sometimes marketing mix models are ideal, sometimes random test designs are, and other times market research is required. By ensuring the right tool is used for the job, organizations can often cut out some of the market research studies that are better handled in marketing mix models and then refocus that money to increase the sample size of market research studies in order to report on individual segments or granular periods of time.

There should be two key outputs for measurement strategy: The *metric playbook* and *development and implementation road map*. The metric playbook acts as a measurement manual of sorts. It includes an overall measurement framework, which is a visual representation of what metrics are important and how they relate to one another. This single framework needs to be understood and adopted by all groups within the organization. The metric playbook should also detail both the definition and calculation method for each metric. The second output is the development and implementation road map, a document that outlines what work is going to take place over time to build the required organizational support, data and data management platform, analytics, and reporting capabilities.

With a proper measurement strategy established early on, your organization will be positioned for success as you develop a world-class financial management platform.

MEASUREMENT AND ATTRIBUTION

Once we know *what* we need to measure, based on the measurement strategy, the next question is *how* to measure. Our ability to accurately do this will affect how well we can answer important questions that are asked every day by business leaders and marketers. What factors helped meet the company's objective? Is it more sales, higher profits, qualified leads, more written policies, higher donations, increased subscriptions, or higher customer value? Which marketing activities caused the customer to make a buying decision? Who or what should get the credit? What influenced the customer to take the desired action? Determining attribution—what contributed to the sale—gives the organization vital information it needs about how to allocate marketing spend in the future.

The need for attribution as part of financial management strategy is not new. Department store pioneer John Wanamaker (1838–1922) is credited with saying, "Half the money I spend on advertising is wasted; the trouble is, I don't know which half." Today's marketer has a far more complex marketplace—and the same question persists.

At its core, attribution is about solving one primary problem: How much marketing credit should be assigned to each marketing activity that has occurred in the past? Once this is determined, the marketer can objectively compare the total cost of a specific marketing tactic to the total incremental marketing impact of that tactic. In this way, a tactic can be judged on cost-effectiveness. This can inform decisions about whether to scale up or scale back on that tactic in the future. Tactics can be evaluated at various levels, ranging from the channel or media level (online display, paid search, social media, e-mail, direct mail, TV, radio, etc.) down to specific campaigns, online placements, or creative treatments.

It is rare to find a company or organization that is not grappling with how to better measure marketing performance. As media proliferates, the problem will only become larger and more complex. Often, when faced with the complexity of measurement, companies opt to take the easy way out and implement simplistic business rules to allocate credit or CMOs delegate important measurement decisions down to each business or marketing group.

The easiest answer to the attribution question is the last-touch method. In this method, 100 percent of marketing credit is given to the marketing touch just prior to conversion. This tends to significantly overvalue touches that happen lower in the conversion funnel and lead to marketing and sales investment decisions that are suboptimal. More effective and accurate attribution methods involve controlled testing and the use of advanced statistical algorithms to determine the appropriate partial credit for each marketing touchpoint.

Another common mistake is to not treat measurement as an enterprise strategy but instead relegate it to individual business and marketing groups. In this case, the organization is robbed of a consistent apples-to-apples view of performance across groups, as different groups calculate metrics in different ways—or worse, use entirely different metrics. Furthermore, marketing performance is often dramatically overstated, as credit for new sales is double or triple counted, or even counted across marketing and sales investments. This problem is easy to detect when you add up the sales created across programs, media, and divisions and they sum to a number that is higher than the actual sales.

So what is the better path? We recommend creating an integrated measurement solution across the enterprise. An integrated solution is one in which we can deliver consistent estimates for each primary metric, across measurement levels and dimensions. These consistent metrics become common currencies, which can then be used across the organization to reduce friction in decision making and, ultimately, create more value.

How do you create an integrated measurement solution? From my experience, the best solutions take both a top-down and a bottom-up approach to measurement. The top-down component is about looking widely, across all media (mass and direct), and accounting for as many internal and external factors as possible that might affect business performance. Other internal factors could be product launches, changes in pricing, service or delivery issues, and positive or negative PR. External factors include such things as the cumulative value of the brand, competitor actions, seasonality, and important macroeconomic trends. Because of the large number of factors, most often companies choose to solve for this through the use of marketing mix models, which look at weekly or monthly aggregated data at a country or regional level. Because these models are based on aggregated data, they rarely can output results at a campaign, placement, or customer level.

Where the top-down measurement methods fall short, the bottom-up methods shine (Figure 7.2). Bottom-up models are built on data that is aggregated at a consumer level (anonymous or identified) by date. Customer interactions across specific media and channel touches are connected back to the customer either by linking and matching data or through probabilistic allocation of credit. These attribution models estimate how much fractional credit for each marketing conversion (such as each sale) was contributed at each touchpoint by taking into account factors such as recency, frequency, type of touch, and consumer engagement, such as ad clicks or site visits. Because these are built at a consumer level, it is relatively easy to roll performance into a specific segment, placement, or campaign. These bottom-up models are then calibrated based on the top-down models to yield a truly comprehensive measurement system.

MetLife is a good example of a company that has worked to develop an integrated measurement solution that is a truly

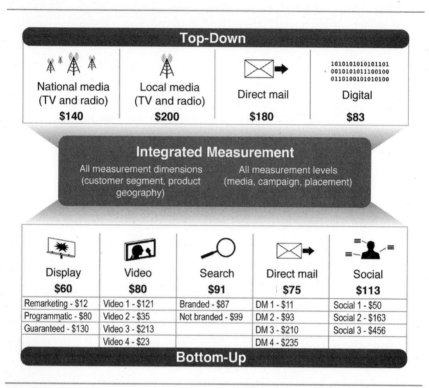

FIGURE 7.2   An Integrated Measurement Approach

competitive asset. In 2011, the company realized that its last-touch method of marketing measurement was not effectively informing decisions across direct, digital, and mass media. Based on a vision of top-down and bottom-up measurement, the company decided to first build out the top-down measurement to help answer important questions about how to allocate budgets across media and segment. To this end, data was collected and organized within a centralized media database. Marketing mix models were built, which suggested that, indeed, budgets were not optimally allocated and that investment in some media, including online display and TV should be increased. Although this insight was valuable, it still left many questions with the planners about how and where to increase these budgets within media. A bottom-up measurement approach based on integrated digital and offline data at a customer level was later implemented. This not only helped MetLife answer important questions about which specific tactics were and were not performing but also led to other insights about how customers were engaging across product lines. For example, the company found that marketing touches aimed at its auto and home product lines were among the primary factors driving sales within its life products.

BUDGET ALLOCATION AND FORECASTING

The measurement discussion so far has been about how to understand the impact of past marketing actions. Although these backward-looking approaches aid the ability to make better decisions going forward, they fall short of helping truly optimize budget planning. If a marketer has an additional million dollars to spend, should that be used to buy more spots on TV in Toronto, target deeper in direct mail deciles, or spend more on targeted Facebook ads? The attribution models might suggest all of these as attractive choices, but truly making the best spend decisions requires forward-looking analytics that can allow the marketer to run scenario optimization exercises and predict marketing impact. How many sales, quotes, prescriptions, subscriptions, or new customers should the marketer expect?

Often, today's marketing organizations have separate teams managing the execution of mass media (TV, radio, print), direct media (direct mail, catalog), and digital media (paid search, display). For some organizations, planning is further fragmented by business unit or product. The result is no cross-channel interplay or understanding of the influence and correlation across channels. Most of these channels are managed by different media managers with unique budgets and little or no incentive to coordinate with the other channels used by their customers. Further complicating this, marketing organizations have different agencies and vendors managing different media channels. These agencies and vendors are often uncoordinated or consider themselves competitive with each other.

So why do brands separate marketing planning by media type? This is partly because mass, direct, and digital media have very different media-buying expertise, planning cycles, supporting technology, and targeting methods. With TV, for example, most planning happens on an annual or semiannual basis, with large purchases often negotiated to target audience demographics, viewing habits, and aggregate purchase patterns. Much of this process happens in an annual TV blitz when marketers get sneak previews of programming for the upcoming year. Contrast this execution process with digital media, where some large guaranteed buys may happen annually but many spend decisions are happening on a monthly or even weekly basis, with daily adjustments and millisecond algorithmic fine-tuning. A marketer might scale back on keywords or change the pacing of the targeted display based on breaking news about a product, a new competitive ad, or myriad other factors that impact program performance. Although distributing marketing responsibilities makes sense from a capability standpoint, it creates unintended consequences.

Consumers today engage with brands by moving seamlessly through channels and across devices. Consumer media consumption habits and purchase behavior can differ significantly across a brand's customer base. The fragmented planning model leads to disconnected brand experiences, inefficient customer contact strategies, and, ultimately, wasted marketing spend.

Today, digital media are creating a wealth of behavioral data that can inform the mass media planning process. Organizations that successfully pivot from a media-centric budget and planning approach to a customer-driven approach will create significant and sustainable competitive advantage in the next five years.

I'm not suggesting a drastic shift in the near term to consolidate all the different marketing functions into a single group or to completely reorganize the company around customer segments. Significant value can be unlocked by enabling marketers at all levels in the organization to not only measure based on customer segment but also plan at the same level. Marketers need the ability to optimize at a media or channel level and also at a much more tactical, campaign, and placement level. This will allow CMOs, vice presidents, and marketing managers to spend smarter and will set the future stage for a realignment of incentives and adjustments to organizational design.

Effective budgeting and planning require three primary analytical capabilities: forecasting, scenario analysis, and constrained optimization.

- *Forecasting* is the ability to predict future performance based on current and future marketing activity and external factors.
- *Scenario analysis* is the ability for marketers to create different forecasts based on marketer-defined future plans and expected future market conditions.
- *Constrained optimization* is the ability to allow the marketer to enter detailed marketing constraints so that mathematical models can generate optimal marketing spend plans.

Predictive analytics is the backbone to each capability. None of these capabilities in and of themselves are new, but their application across all measurement levels and dimensions in the campaign planning process, enabled by customer-level data, is revolutionary. The goal is to give marketers the information needed at the speed at which they make decisions. And it gives marketers visibility into how these decisions will affect the broader ecosystem of marketing activity, driving acquisition of high-value customers and maximizing the value of existing customers.

A major pharmaceutical company needed a holistic measurement and planning approach to understand the relative impact of consumer- and physician-oriented marketing efforts, thereby enabling them to make better decisions. The company has two well-known brands that spent more than $150 million in annual direct-to-consumer marketing and more than $200 million in physician-targeted marketing and sales force.

Merkle was asked to help the company understand the incremental impact of historical marketing efforts on new prescriptions, as well as provide tools to drive physician-level spend decisions. The solution was to leverage multiple sources of data at different levels, including physician-level promotional activity, physician and managed care specialty data, and geographical information. The modeling data included two years' worth of data and more than 400,000 physicians, or 9.6 million records (400,000 physicians × 24 months). The output of this project was a scenario-planning and optimization tool that allowed the marketers to understand how to allocate budgets across media tactics and which tactics were most effective for each physician, be it increased e-mail contacts or more in-person visits from sales reps (Figure 7.3).

Within just three months of implementing the tool, marketers had generated cost savings of more than $5 million with the same level of new prescription volume.

VALIDATION

Evolution to more sophisticated measurement and planning systems inherently creates perceived winners and losers. Challenges to long-held beliefs and marketer intuition naturally arise, which leads to questioning of the new methods and potentially, if left unchecked, to the undermining of the change initiative. In addition, sometimes analysts get it wrong as they deploy new measurement and planning capabilities. For these reasons, it is critical that validation be an integral part of any financial management strategy. Simply stated, validation is the process of thoroughly vetting results through comprehensive quality control (QC) and controlled testing. It often strikes me that,

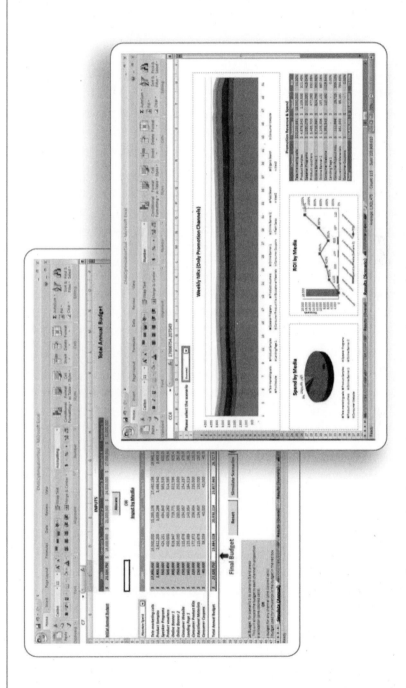

FIGURE 7.3 Scenario Planning and Optimization Tool

in the name of validation, a pharmaceutical company will use placebos on a hold-out sample—potentially affecting the life of the patient—for the sake of advancing a drug approval. That same company will balk at the idea of pulling media spend from a given metropolitan statistical area (MSA) to test the viability of an ad campaign for fear of losing one exposure. Companies need to put the value of testing and validation into perspective. When done well, it will drive confidence and belief in the measurement and forecasting, leading to increased adoption in the enterprise.

Effective validation requires three elements, namely, a validation plan, an ability to implement validation insights back into the measurement and planning system, and finally a normative database that documents validation results over time.

A validation plan requires a step-by-step validation approach to ensure that estimated historical and future metrics are correctly calculated. Newly estimated metrics should be shown side by side with the metrics the organization is accustomed to seeing (old way) to create transparency and build confidence in the new approach. Controlled testing plays a central role in the validation and evolution of any measurement solution. When a sophisticated attribution solution is created, there are many ways to make mistakes. More often than not, important data are wrong, incomplete, or missing altogether, and the analyst is left to do his or her best to overcome such limitations. Errors can also be introduced during the analytical process if models are not validated correctly or poor assumptions are made. A rigorous, continuous testing approach can suss out errors and bad assumptions, and the results should be used to recalibrate the underlying measurement system. Testing is not a one-time process as the new system is introduced, but rather an ongoing discipline that will regularly improve the measurement system. Significant hard costs and opportunity costs are associated with testing, so organizations need to be smart about where they focus testing resources, with priority given to areas where spend is significant and where the measurement system results are suspect or challenged. Finally, forecasted results based on plans should be systematically compared against actual results on an ongoing basis to further build confidence in and improve the solution.

Invariably, the validation process highlights shortcomings and improvement points in the current financial measurement system. The system must be flexible enough to allow these insights to be incorporated back into the system. Expectations should be set beforehand within the organization that this is a natural part of the process. For example, outside testing may show that new display media metrics are inflated by 10 percent. As the financial management system is updated to reflect this, it will further establish confidence in the system.

Finally, insights that are gleaned through this validation process must not be lost. I can't tell you how many times we've seen companies glean important insights through validation, only to have them disappear within an ocean of results, never surviving beyond the immediate team who drove the testing. The result is costly, with potentially valuable resources spent retesting or, worse, with the organization failing to enact lasting change based on the testing outcomes. The solution to this is to methodically track all tests parameters and results within a database that will outlive the immediate project team.

After a major marketing mix modeling project was completed for a top technology company, many within the organization questioned some important findings from the effort. One such finding was that freestanding print inserts (FSIs) in newspapers were performing at a significantly higher level than the company could measure based strictly on direct calls to the 800 number printed on the inserts. Marketers could not believe this finding. In fact, FSIs were scheduled to be removed from the marketing budget altogether once the current contracts expired. Because of these FSI results, all of the results of the measurement project were questioned.

To address the doubters, the company first did a thorough review of the entire data collection and modeling process leading to the finding. This was followed by two matched market blackout tests where markets in the control did not receive FSIs while other similar markets did. The results from the two tests validated the recommendations from the models and were added to an Excel spreadsheet that contained results from all tests that had been performed during that year. This gave the organization confidence to not only reinstate the FSI program but to do so at higher levels of funding.

This FSI testing was part of a larger and highly structured media testing and improvement initiative within the company. Marketers would bring testing needs and ideas that required cross-channel coordination to a centralized measurement group. Many of these test requests required coordination across media to execute. As such, this group was responsible for the following:

- Intake of test requests
- Estimation of the potential impact based on cost savings or increased profit and ease of execution of the test
- Review of the library of prior testing and results to determine whether the test was necessary
- Ultimate prioritization, scheduling, and coordination of tests (many test ideas were killed based on evaluation of benefit and cost of executing test)
- Test design and documentation
- Test analysis, sharing of results, and documentation of results

The benefit to this structured approach was that the marketer was able to focus its limited testing resources on those strategic initiatives that would have the most impact, execute more testing overall (through centralized planning), and reduce the number of failed tests. In addition, by having a central library of tests and results, the company was able to help new team members ramp up faster and avoid recreating the wheel as they learn from their predecessors' tests.

SUMMARY

Effective financial management is the backbone of an effective cCRM strategy. It is the mechanism that allows the organization to learn from the past and make better decisions in the future. For it to be most effective, it cannot simply be an ad hoc process that is done once a year as part of a planning exercise or something that is delegated out to each business unit to solve. It must be enterprise-wide, and it must be built with a blend of integrated technology and analytics so that marketers can get the answers they need when they need them—whether making decisions about adjustments to marketing budgets on a quarterly basis or driving daily optimizations within digital media. Companies that have an effective measurement strategy, sophisticated measurement and attribution practices, meticulous budget allocation and forecasting methods, and reliable validation processes can create sustainable competitive separation and value.

THE HEART OF THE MATTER

The following central takeaways from this chapter should be considered when developing your financial measurement strategy:

- As you implement the measurement structure for your cCRM approach, remember that a broad redefinition of metrics and how they are calculated affects all areas of the organization, including existing processes and compensation plans. It's therefore critical to not only get the math right but also properly manage the cultural change to ensure adoption across groups and at all levels. It is essential to have alignment from the CMO and potentially CFO.
- A measurement strategy must contain five essential components: a complete set of metrics, consistent execution, applicability across all measurement levels, applicability across all measurement dimensions, and flawless methodology. These

components are articulated in the metric playbook and planned out in the development and implementation road map.

- Methodologies must be clearly defined and consistently executed to determine which marketing activities had the largest bearing on customer behavior. Measurement of results and attribution of those results to the most impactful touchpoints are vital to the future allocation of budget dollars.

TWO

cCRM OPERATING MODEL

Chapter 8 Infrastructure and Process

Dismantling the Silos That Hinder

We've built databases for more than 20 years, and we've gotten pretty good at it from a technical perspective. They function just as promised. They collect, format, standardize, comingle, and store the data from multiple customer interactions. And yet, for all they are capable of doing, why are so many databases underused? Why do they fail to yield their full potential value? My belief is that the people in the organization who own the database function often don't have the right support or even a total vision of the enormity of the power that it wields.

When a $5 billion company sets out to build a $2 million database, often it can be a relatively junior-level decision. I believe that is at the heart of the problem. If the database isn't built with executive-level buy-in—or even a mandate—it will be underused across the enterprise. These days, everyone knows they must have a customer database to do business, so they often develop one simply because it's the thing to do. "Build it, and they will come," with no forward-looking plan for the kind of results the database can create and how they can integrate it into the business. They are so focused on the bells and whistles that they don't consider what those features can mean to the overall business strategy.

The bottom line is that before the database is commissioned, you must outline the expected customer experience at all touchpoints and the required functionality to support it. Executive sponsorship must be established to ensure enterprise support, and leadership must understand the big picture of what the database is expected to do. Only then can you define the technological infrastructure to enable it. Chapter 9 will delve deeper into the concept of executive sponsorship and the level of involvement required to distinguish it from mere permission.

With the right organizational approach, infrastructure and process together enable capabilities that deliver the cCRM vision and strategy for the enterprise. Applications, encoded business rules and analytical frameworks, and data included in infrastructure all drive processes, whereas process puts infrastructure to work. Almost anything can be accomplished once simply through the heroics of the dedicated few. But sustained, consistent execution requires supporting infrastructure. When aligned in an effective platform, they are a critical underpinning for cCRM at scale and effective drivers of value and marketplace differentiation. The goal is to simplify process and make the infrastructure do as much of the work as possible while retaining flexibility.

Faced with an operating gap, wherein infrastructure and process are not aligned, marketers have few options:

- *Do without.* They can pursue the next best strategy that can be successfully performed with the capabilities allowed by existing infrastructure and process. This tactic is suboptimal and causes the organization to suffer hidden opportunity costs.
- *Change the process.* They can pursue manual workaround processes to fill the operating gap. This tactic is limited by the complexity of the task as well as affordability of the incremental labor.

- *Extend the infrastructure.* Add functionality, whether built, bought, or rented. This will create cCRM capabilities that can operate at scale. But it takes resources (time, money, and bandwidth) to implement.

Ideally, marketers should seek a platform that automates cCRM complexity, including continuous improvement and learning.

Consider the example of a leading grocery retailer operating under multiple brands throughout the United States. Its customer program is a new marketing platform and coupon delivery system that enables shoppers to receive targeted and personalized digital promotional offers and communications, both online and via a smartphone app. It promises a powerful, bidirectional, one-to-one communication with each shopper, with the goal of driving customer loyalty. Despite this communication channel, without the infrastructure to create and manage offers to increasingly finer consumer segments, this grocer is limited in its ability to fully exploit the channel at scale.

By now most organizations have made significant investments in marketing technologies that support their processes. Many of these investments have been made with the view that they would improve the way the organization can communicate with its end consumers. The challenge with many of these investments is that although they had a notion of the right business goals, those goals were initially set without an understanding of how the infrastructure and process truly work together to enable capabilities that will ultimately deliver the value behind cCRM. This problem is further compounded by rapid evolution in channel and media technologies and the explosion of big data.

In today's terms, here is how marketing infrastructure and process are coming into play and how we must look to adjust our view of them to create platforms that will enable cCRM. In the simplest form, we can plot marketing data management capabilities along two axes. Referring to Figure 8.1, the first axis

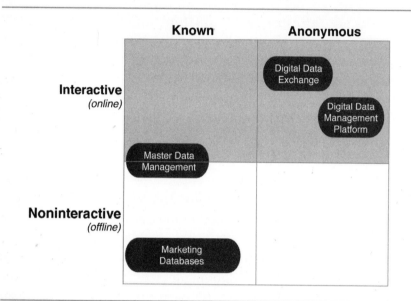

FIGURE 8.1 Technology Matrix

represents whether the consumer with whom we are communicating is known or anonymous. The second axis is based on the degree to which this communication is interactive or noninteractive. Other axes could be considered as well, but these two represent the major stumbling blocks for many organizations.

The first continuum addresses the consumer's identity. Identity in the marketing world is no longer defined as simply name and address. The consumer can have both direct identifiers, such as name, address, and phone number, and anonymous identifiers, such as e-mail address, cookie, device ID, or IP address. The number of potential identifiers is evolving. As we see the role of the cookie diminish over time, we will see newer identity attributes such as device fingerprints and the next evolution of the IP address, IPv6, begin to move to the forefront. In the identity continuum, you will find that most marketing capabilities excel at leveraging either known or anonymous identity attributes. They often claim they can do the other, but this is generally not the case. Infrastructure and process born from digital marketing typically excel in the anonymous world and have limited capabilities with offline identity attributes, and traditional marketing infrastructure and process excel with offline identity attributes but struggle to incorporate anonymous attributes. This chasm between the offline and online identity presents a significant challenge to cCRM.

The second continuum is focused on noninteractive and interactive communications with a consumer. Many view the interactive world as the digital media and channels and the noninteractive world as everything else. In reality, this thinking is what creates a barrier to true cross-channel marketing. We define interactive marketing as any communication that relies on existing data housed by the marketing system to be combined with data generated at the point in time the consumer is addressing the channel in order make a decision regarding how to best communicate with that consumer. For example, you go to your favorite website to look for a new computer. After examining a few items, you noticed the banner ads on the side pannel become more focused on a set of offers related to computers that interest you and are in your price range. In the background what has occurred is that the cookie and mouse clicks from your current shopping session are being collected and combined with data from your past purchases to construct a compelling offer for a new computer. This same example could be applied to an inbound call to the call center, where the same set of infrastructure and process should construct the appropriate offer for each of these interactions.

If we lay out the two axes and plot a few common marketing-related capabilities, we can quickly see the gaps in the current set that need to be overcome.

The digital components are focused in the anonymous, interactive channels and media, and these components do not provide a clean way to leverage the capabilities across the entire interactive world. The traditional marketing solutions are too focused in the identifiable world, and they don't consider enough of the anonymous side, which in turn leaves out much of the digital universe. Further complicating this is that ownership of the solutions is split across different marketing departments, digital and direct, and IT.

When we implement a cCRM strategy, we must focus on infrastructure and processes that allow us to connect interactions across both anonymous and known identities and to manage the totality of the marketing assets in a holistic environment that can inform all channels and media, interactive and noninteractive. Failure to do so will only create new marketing and data silos that will limit your ability to provide a connected experience to the consumer.

THE SIX CORE CAPABILITIES

Six core infrastructure and process capabilities comprise the cCRM platform (Figure 8.2):

- *Connected consumer profile:* the ability to source, capture, cleanse, link, and integrate all data in the organization's CRM data strategy and recognize prospects and customers at points of interaction regardless of the channel or media
- *Longitudinal view of consumer interactions:* the ability to understand the sequence of consumer engagements for insight into cross-channel attribution and to support media and channel marketing actions
- *Insights platform:* the ability to make the enterprise's information assets available and part of normal business operations with access to the right level of data, to the right users, and with the right tools to enable cCRM decisions
- *Cross-channel marketing enablement:* the ability to make informed decisions regarding marketing mix optimization and implement actions that improve cCRM performance through holistic marketing mix management

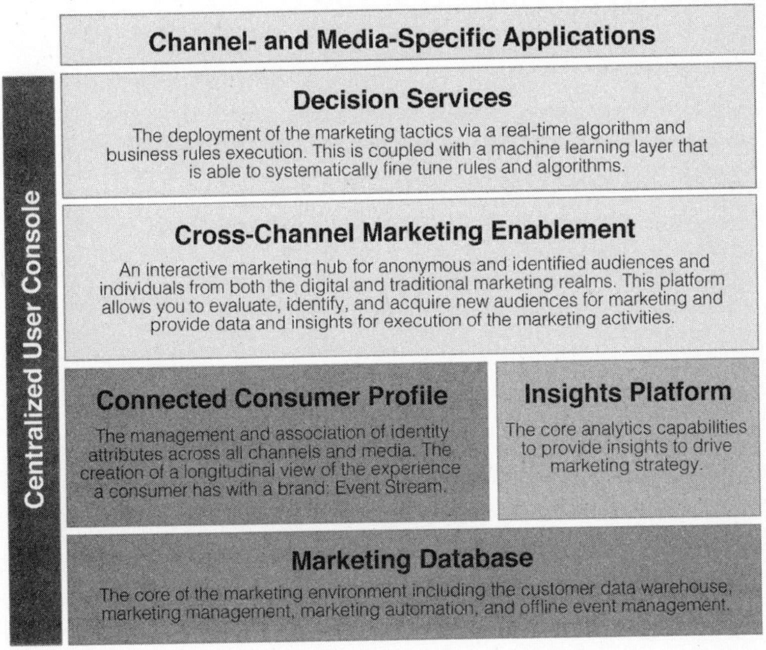

FIGURE 8.2 The cCRM Enablement Platform

- *Decision services:* the ability to support all interactions and make decisions across campaigns regarding customer-level offers, personalization, and delivery, regardless of channel or media
- *Centralized user console:* the ability to make the cCRM platform accessible for configuring inputs for marketing actions and monitoring outputs for driving decisions around cCRM campaign execution.

The cCRM platform is enabled by process and enterprise-class technologies and embedded analytical frameworks that support relevant consumer interactions and drive meaningful marketing results. Each capability is integral to the infrastructure and process, and deficiencies in any capability weaken the entire platform. Our focus will be on the actual capabilities, not their physical implementation or the specific related processes.

CONNECTED CONSUMER PROFILE

The foundational capability for success in any CRM platform is the ability to collect, cleanse, and associate all data to a single consumer. In the past, this effort was largely a function of rationalizing names and addresses down to an individual. As time progressed and the number of addressable channels and media increased, the identity of an individual began to evolve and contain many more attributes. To bring this to life, let's look at a series of interactions that a single consumer could have with a brand and identify the variety of attributes that could be used to construct an individual's identity (Figure 8.3).

These myriad identity attributes have to be rationalized to identify the behaviors of a single person, and at different times

Interaction	Channel or Media	Identity Attributes
Promotional offer for a discounted rate on car insurance	Direct mail	Name, address
Visits website to evaluate insurance offerings and signs up for an e-mail newsletter	Website	1st-party cookie, e-mail address
Visits news website and receives a banner ad promoting insurance	Website	3rd party cookie
Calls 800 number to discuss insurance offerings	Call center	Phone number, name
Receives newsletter	E-mail	1st-party cookie
Searches for insurance offerings and clicks link in search results	Search	1st-party cookie
Completes online quote	Website	1st-party cookie, name, address, phone number
Uses Facebook Connect button to log in	Social media	1st-party cookie, e-mail address, social network user ID
Visits mobile site for information	Mobile website	Device ID, setting (used to create a device fingerprint), cookie

FIGURE 8.3   Consumer Interaction Matrix

this person may be anonymous or known to the brand. This rationalization of identity is needed to develop contextual, relevant, and personalized experiences for each consumer. In the absence of this, everyone would always be viewed as a new person.

This foundational capability must be built as a learning business system. The platform must be continually collecting, evaluating, and reevaluating every identity attribute to construct a map of all identity attributes and their relationship to one another. There are four key components of the platform to construct a connected consumer profile:

- *Data quality mechanisms:* Every attribute considered must be evaluated to determine whether it meets a specific set of criteria to determine its quality. These criteria can range from expected values and frequencies to salacious word identification. Good examples of this are the use of postal files to determine the validity of a street address or the verification of an e-mail addresses construction (identifier followed by @ and then a domain). The key is to prevent the introduction of bad data into the system. This is where the adage "garbage in means garbage out" comes into play.

- *Associative rules and algorithms:* The next key to the connected profile is the set of associative rules and algorithms used to construct the map of an individual's identity. This is where the learning part of the business system is working. Every time a new identity attribute is introduced to the platform, it must be evaluated against the other identity attributes to determine whether an association can be made. For example, you sign up for an e-mail newsletter and browse the store website. At this point you are known by your e-mail address and a cookie. You then call the call center to purchase a new computer. They collect your name, address, phone number, and e-mail address. As you can see from this simple example, all of these components would be introduced into the platform and it would be able to ultimately determine that the e-mail addresses captured through the website and the call center are the same. In turn, this would allow the marketer to associate the online activity with the purchase in the call center. Unfortunately, all of the associations are not this straightforward.

In most cases these association are rules based (in the preceding scenario, for example, if e-mail address equals e-mail address then associate the identity attributes), but in certain situations these associations are based on more sophisticated algorithms. Take, for instance, a device finger-print. A device fingerprint is created by evaluating the specific settings of a browser against an algorithm to determine the likelihood that this browser is one that has interacted with the website before. As we see certain identity attributes, such as the cookie, diminish in prominence, these types of identity mechanisms begin to take front stage. Our systems of associ-ation must be ready to collect and evaluate these new identity attributes.

- *Identity references:* Most organizations do not possess enough data to appropriately associate all identity attributes; therefore, they must leverage outside sources to better inform the asso-ciative rules. In the case of name and address, this may entail leveraging postal files to understand when a person moves to a different address, or it may be the use of e-mail databases that provide associations to physical identity attributes or other digital identity attributes. These publicly available reference bases become key players in maintaining accurate associations in the data.

- *Identity attribute governance:* The final component deals with the governance of identity attributes. Over time, certain attributes diminish in value to the associative rules or have limited use because of regulatory constraints. The business system must be able to understand and act according to these characteristics to prevent the inappropriate usage of certain identity attributes. The inability of the business system to govern attribute usage can introduce bad data into the system or yield monetary consequences because of inappropriate data usage.

LONGITUDINAL VIEW OF INTERACTIONS

Once we have created a map of the identity, the next step is to rationalize the different experiences an individual has with a brand. This capability must be able to create a chronological series of events based on every engagement a consumer has with a brand. These events are direct mail pieces sent to the consumer's house, retail store purchases, displayed banner ads, Facebook likes, e-mails received, content viewed on the website, and even location information from the mobile phone. This chronological set of events is called the event stream.

The goal of the event stream is to enable the development of insights that will allow a marketer to more effectively communicate with a single individual. It allows us to get answers for questions such as:

- What series of events led to a purchase?
- How do specific segments like to engage the brand?
- Is there any value in leveraging certain channels and media to communicate with some individuals?
- What information was an individual exposed to before his or her next experience?

Armed with answers to these types of questions, we are able to affect the next step in the consumer's experience, and when we act to affect the next step, it will have relevance and context that can be leveraged to develop personalized content for the individual. Ultimately, the goal is to better inform, accelerate conversion, create loyalty, or win back the consumer.

The identity map and the event stream are the two capabilities that create the keystone for the rest of the platform. These capabilities are the basis for enabling customer centricity. Through the identity map, all data is associated with a single individual. This allows us to understand with whom we are speaking. With the event stream we are able to better understand how a consumer engages with us. These capabilities allow us to develop richer segments, better understand the return on marketing investments, and maintain individualized relationships with our consumers.

LEVERAGING THE IDENTITY MAP AND THE EVENT STREAM

Organizations that are successful in creating both the identity map and the event stream—and have the ability to link them across the online and offline world—have realized significant gains. One of Merkle's technology clients sends millions of catalogs and e-mails worldwide and has millions of visitors to its websites. The company's success in developing a connected view of the consumer and a longitudinal view of the consumer's experience has yielded numerous benefits:

- Having integrated e-mail campaigns drawing on a large audience of individuals linked to site activity has enabled the company to improve the relevance of those e-mail messages. This has yielded incremental annual revenue of $3 million.
- The company has seen a 13 to 15 percent increase in lift from predictive models once site data was added into the mix.
- Projected incremental annual revenue of $10 million is attributed to improved product recommendations through the use of the event stream.
- The technology company has been able to derive more actionable insights in areas that were previously beyond its capabilities. This entails better understanding around device usage and device preferences.

Although these capabilities alone do not provide these returns, they do represent the foundational component that must be executed effectively in order to be successful with any other marketing activity.

INSIGHTS PLATFORM

The insights platform represents a key convergence point in the enabling cCRM infrastructure. It's a critical component to realizing a holistic CRM capability. It becomes a driver for every aspect of the platform, providing insights for traditional direct campaigns, real-time personalized digital campaigns, programs driven through a data management platform (DMP), and corporate-level decision support for determining what to maximize and what to minimize. This component leverages an analytical approach to drive meaningful marketing results.

The insights platform lies at the intersection of data, strategy, analytics, and technology. In today's digital world the insights platform is where the line between technology and analytics begins to blur. This component calls for a dedicated infrastructure to support analytics, which is often overlooked when organizations build out their CRM infrastructure. And it is much more than a collection point for disparate data or a dumping zone for raw data. The role of the insights platform is to put analytical insight into an "actioning" context.

To realize the full benefit of the insights platform takes balance between the right technology tools and the right configuration of data, analytic methods, and supporting processes. Herein lies the need for a balance between art and science to make data actionable. The key is to arrange data in a way in which insight is readily available and action is easily enabled.

Consider a hypothetical example of a brand launching a new product through social channels. To gauge success, a framework is designed in the insights platform for transforming the available raw social data into a more meaningful and actionable structure. A social activity aggregate is designed for individual-level data that facilitate insight generation and access for audience selections that inform ongoing dialog. Derived attributes at the consumer level are created to profile and gauge the level of interaction and interest, such as:

- Number of social networks
- Number of positive, neutral, and negative mentions about the product
- Number of followers/friends
- Number of mentions of specific keywords
- Level of social activity in category (high/medium/low)
- Engagement segments (content consumer, active responder, sharer, contributor)

These metrics are insightful and actionable. Next, a targeting strategy is implemented to maximize impact by engaging in relevant dialog with consumers using the segments to personalize communications. They may look something like this:

- *Content consumer:* one-way, information-based dialog
- *Active responder:* offer-based relationship engagement
- *Sharer:* promote consumer as an effective broadcast tower
- *Contributor:* leverage to stimulate "community" interest

Although simple, this example shows how raw data is transformed into derivations that are embedded into the platform for ready access. This type of embedded framework in the insights platform becomes even more interesting when advanced analytics are leveraged to create predictive consumer attributes, such as an opportunity score that predicts future value.

Consider another hypothetical example involving digital engagement. Assume a company monitors consumer activity on branded websites by leveraging a tagging strategy that tracks high-value actions (HVAs). HVAs include actions such as registration on the site, video views, profile updates, and content shares or downloads. These actions are translated into a conglomerate engagement score at the consumer level. In addition, a directional indicator is derived that indicates whether the consumer is trending up, trending down, or staying flat in terms of engagement actions over a rolling three-month period. The framework allows the organization to monitor activity, serve relevant content, reward those who are increasing in engagement, proactively reach out to save those that are in decline, and model look-alikes to obtain more high-value consumers and promote new offerings.

Key Ingredients of an Insights Platform

The infrastructure and process ingredients for a successful insights platform include the following:

- *Intelligent design:* Design smart analytical frameworks to go beyond raw data and make the insight apparent and actionable, supporting the next best action.
- *Customer-centric focus:* Design the insight platform to track down to the customer level, which is foundational for cCRM. This provides the ability to roll up to the segment level or beyond while also supporting the granularity of the customer.
- *Flexible analytical tools:* Leverage enterprise-class analytical tools that provide analytical horsepower as the business grows and evolves. SAS and R are a couple of options that will grow with your business as you move up the sophistication scale.
- *Operationalized analytic processes:* A word of caution: Don't ignore the operational aspects of managing an insights platform. It takes rigor and specialization to automate and embed analytics into the platform. Analytics or technology talent working in isolation will not likely fulfill this mission. It takes collaboration between these two disciplines to make it work. Running analytics in isolation simply won't scale in today's real-time world. Bulk data transfers out to a proprietary analytical package for batch scoring every day/week/month will no longer keep up with the speed of customers and the agility required to satisfy their needs and expectations. The insights

platform and all supporting processes have to be nimble and real-time capable with access to current, updated information.

- *Processing horsepower for big data:* Couple your enterprise analytical tools with a processing environment to handle massive amounts of data. One without the other will result in a suboptimal environment. For example, the analytical package R coupled with an open-source Hadoop/Hive environment will scale by utilizing commodity hardware. This will accommodate the explosion of data volumes in digital sources and provide performance and affordable scalability as the business expands and becomes dependent on the CRM infrastructure. This type of open environment also provides agility through a cloud-based option as well. Without an environment like the one described, you can find yourself backed into a corner if processing throughput fails to keep up with execution demand.

CROSS-CHANNEL MARKETING ENABLEMENT

There is no doubt that consumers today are increasing touch-point interactions across channels. The preceding social and site examples become even more powerful when combined to create a holistic, cross-channel view of consumer interactions for a brand. A modern CRM platform is required to integrate cross-channel views and to execute seamlessly across all channels where consumers are engaged. Bottom line: Cross-channel marketing enablement is a requirement leveled on marketers by consumers, whether they are ready or not!

Our team truly believes customer-centric marketing requires a sturdy cross-channel measurement capability embedded within the insights platform in the form of cross-channel attribution. This solution flips the paradigm of going deep within a single channel and driving channel-specific goals. It rises up a level and focuses on how the consumer actually engages across channels, assigning credit accurately based on conversion, and optimizing channel activity based on consumer behavior.

But the infrastructure to support cross-channel attribution is not trivial and represents another point where technology and analytics converge to support a holistic CRM capability.

Key Ingredients of Cross-Channel Marketing Enablement

The successful infrastructure and process ingredients for cross-channel attribution and marketing enablement include the following:

- *A compiled event stream:* The event stream created in a solution such as Merkle's Connected Recognition (CR) process solves a large portion of the data puzzle for attribution. It arranges digital and direct interactions in a longitudinal fashion and serves as input into the cross-channel attribution process. However, we also need to represent traditional offline media such as print and direct response TV in order to have a holistic event stream. A compiled event stream for a consumer or prospect experience might look like this:

  1. A direct mail piece is delivered to a prospective consumer.
  2. The consumer is shown a display ad the next day.
  3. The consumer then sees a 30-second TV spot with an 800 number.
  4. Minutes later, the consumer calls the 800 number.
  5. A follow-up e-mail is sent with the requested information.
  6. The consumer opens the e-mail 5 hours later.
  7. Four days later, the consumer clicks on a branded paid search ad.
  8. Fifteen minutes later, the consumer completes a quote request.

  In addition to this engagement data, additional information for the modeling process that is common in the event stream includes cookie ID, date and timestamp, user software data (browser ID, version, and operating system [OS]), locale data (country ID, state, and city), and event specifics (site page ID, campaign ID, ad IDs for creative type and size).

Last, the event stream data needs to be reformatted or flattened out to serve as an input that is effective for the attribution modeling process. The event stream is typically aggregated to the consumer or cookie level, with fields representing the longitudinal event stream bucketed into a flat record that's conducive as input into most modeling tools.

- *Sophisticated attribution modeling and analytics:* The analytics required for true cross-channel attribution modeling are complex. The model ideally uses each touchpoint's channel, timing, content, placement, sequence, and other factors to estimate the touchpoint's share of credit for a conversion. Furthermore, model validation is important. In addition to the fractional attribution modeling approach described, it is a best practice to also generate comparative models.

  ○ Last event or last click model: Full, 100 percent credit for conversion is given to the last marketing touchpoint before conversion.

  ○ Proportional model: Equal credit is given to marketing touchpoints the consumer saw before conversion.

  Both of these models are common comparison approaches. In addition, there are other important modeling characteristics for proper cross-channel attribution:

  ○ Timing and recency effects: A model applies exponential decay to all touchpoints based on the time since conversion and controls for recency of impressions using estimated decay factory over time (similar to ad-stock in media mix).

  ○ Repeated touchpoints: This process removes duplicate touchpoints within a reasonable time period and applies exponential diminishing returns to multiple touchpoints.

  ○ Overestimating: This process controls typical overestimation of search by using a two-stage model: Stage 1 predicts search clicks from other media, such as display; stage 2 uses residual from stage 1 to represent paid search, subtracting out other media driving search.

- ○ Principle component analysis (PCA): Use of PCA reduces the dimensionality of data, resulting in better model results.
- ○ Retargeting effect: Subsequent impressions for users who visit a site are tagged and entered into the model.
- ○ Validation: As mentioned earlier, validate, but also be sensitive to bootstrap samples and week-to-week variability.
- ○ Attribution formula: Transform impression weights into likelihood to convert at user level, with predicted probability.

  When performed properly, attribution modeling can provide rich insights for optimizing channel mix. Granular insights such as the prevalent OS of consumers most likely to convert, the degree of channel overlap among converters, and channel interplay insights, such as the degree to which display is driving paid search and video, can help optimize execution.

- *Generation of actionable output:* The outputs from cross-channel attribution should be standardized output feeds that provide insight back to ad servers, DSPs, websites, and search engines, for example, helping dictate changes for better optimization. Outputs for decisions should also include the following views in a visually oriented business intelligence (BI) tool:
  - ○ Performance results (actual versus planned)
  - ○ Media targeting recommendations
  - ○ Channel optimization recommendations
  - ○ Media mix budget allocation and planning insights

  Last, these outputs should ideally be served back to media placement and usage functions in real time via a data services layer enabled by an application program interface (API) or Web service capability.

CENTRALIZED DECISION SERVICES

This component completes the "last mile" portion of the cCRM infrastructure by addressing consumer interaction points. In a building block fashion, this component complements the insights platform and cross-channel attribution solution by providing the execution engine for managing consumer interactions. Centralized decision services supports all interactions and makes decisions across campaigns regarding consumer-level offers, personalization, and delivery, regardless of channel or media. The focus is to deliver the desired outcomes by drawing from the available insight and managing the interaction in the most relevant, meaningful way. The outcome could be a positive consumer response such as a sale, a satisfied customer, a new customer, a returning customer, or a customer who is no longer upset with the brand and is willing to give them another chance.

We are prescribing a central hub for decisions that govern customer interactions. Too often, interaction decisions are made at the end of a channel "spoke" with no regard for the interactions of the other spokes. For example, my airline recently sent me a "Get Away" promotional e-mail while I was in the airport experiencing a 4-hour flight delay. In this case the e-mail spoke was not integrated with the operational spoke, resulting in an annoying customer experience and a wasted effort on the part of the brand. I was left wondering if the airline really knew what my experience was with the brand—or if they even cared!

A centralized decision capability will guard against decisions in isolation that lead to broken consumer experiences. It abstracts decisions out of channel or spoke technologies and centralizes them into a hub for holistic decision management. Given today's proliferation of channels and the fast-moving digital world, this centralized component is critical for best-in-class CRM execution. Without it, the cCRM efforts can backfire, resulting in a negative effect, like my airline experience.

Key Ingredients of Centralized Decision Services

The successful infrastructure ingredients for centralized decision services include the following:

- *Rules and decision engine:* A dedicated decision engine capability is required. The landscape for these tools is evolving fast. Traditional players in the campaign management space, such as Unica and Neolane offer a module for real-time decisioning and personalization. Emerging players that are pure-play tool providers, such as Zementis and Causata, are two examples with decision management and rules engines that promote the importance of taking an analytical approach to driving personalization. Evolving players that have changed their business models and morphed into the space of personalization and decision management, such as FICO, have a personalization engine called Retail Action Manager that promotes the promise of providing personalization in action. ExactTarget started as an e-mail service provider but has focused recently on expanding beyond e-mail into cross-channel decision and personalization offerings.

  Another trend has emerged as traditional database vendors work to embed analytics at the core of their solutions for in-database analytics. For example, Oracle has extended into real-time decision capabilities with its RTD offering, which supports real-time decision and personalization capabilities. And Merkle and other CRM agencies are evolving their marketing service provider capabilities into real-time decision and personalization. The CRM agencies represent a nice option for companies looking for a full-service solution that can be surrounded by other supporting CRM capabilities.

- *Open environment for omni-channel connectivity:* Information (an offer, a message, a suggestion) should be available across all channels to support a diverse customer base. For example, a customer with a preference for mobile communications should receive mobile messages. A customer with a preference for offline should receive messages via a call center or direct mail.

- *Testing and machine learning:* An effective decision and personalization solution will provide an agile way to test, assess, and adjust for continuous learning. Testing and incremental improvements are critical to maintaining a learning algorithm. More specifically, the decision engine for cCRM should have analytic models that continue to learn. This represents machine learning, which is the process of looking through data for patterns. Instead of extracting data for human interpretation, machine learning uses data to improve the program's own understanding. Machine learning programs detect patterns in data and adjust program actions. For example, Facebook's News Feed changes according to a user's personal interactions with other users. If a user frequently tags a friend in photos, writes on his wall or "likes" his links, the News Feed will show more of that friend's activity in the user's News Feed, presuming a closeness between the two.

A common CRM self-learning example is the ability to arrive at the "next best offer" for individual consumers. The models draw from consumer-level patterns to predict a series of subsequent actions that maximize responsiveness and consumer engagement. The less desirable alternative is a one-size-fits-all modeling approach, which ignores segment- and consumer-level nuances.

In an airline case, customers instantly began blogging on a popular frequent flyer blog site about the real-time personalization and offer "decisioning" that was served to them in their browser. The interaction among customers and comments provided validation that the differentiation, timeliness, and content were well received. One blogger commented that he appreciated getting his offer in real time as opposed to waiting for it in the "snail-mail." Another blogger commented that his offer was different, bringing attention to the differentiation that was driven by a lifetime value analytical model. A third blogger commented that he did not receive an offer, but he hadn't flown the airline in quite some time and was "not surprised" at the nonoffer.

This represents an example of segmented personalization, real-time centralized decisioning, and the airline's efforts to spend its marketing dollars on customers with the highest likelihood of rewarding them with incremental/repeat business.

AARP is another company that is effectively leveraging a centralized decision service for cross-channel execution. AARP presents customized offers to visitors on its Health page (www .aarp.org/health); these offers are contextually aware and customized based on the member or prospect's profile. It works as follows:

1. The consumer goes to the AARP site.
2. She logs in as a user (known or anonymous).
3. A real-time Web service retrieves her profile.
4. A rules engine fires and determines the appropriate/eligible offer for the individual.
5. The offer is rendered in real time while the consumer in still within her Web session.

A typical day can yield roughly 11,000 anonymous visitors and more than 1,000 members who are served relevant customized offers for interactions in real time using Merkle's member profile database and real-time decision engine powered by Unica Interact. The success of this program has driven AARP to leverage this capability across various online properties including its contact centers.

CENTRALIZED USER CONSOLE

Last is the centralized user console. We live in an increasing self-service world, and this trend applies to marketers as well. The cCRM landscape is a diverse and complex environment. A centralized user console is required to administer and control all aspects of the platform, provide configuration inputs for marketing actions, and provide access to insights for monitoring outcomes and driving decisions around CRM execution. The access console is a single access point that provides visibility and transparency to all aspects of the system.

Key Ingredients of a Centralized User Console

A successful design for the console includes the following components (Figure 8.4):

- *Dashboard:* Gain access to visualization tools that provide direct insight into program performance results and trends over time.
- *Media targeting:* Select media targeting parameters, set thresholds, and add/remove constraints.
- *Customer segmentation:* Access segment detail, apply recommendations to audiences, and review results by segment.
- *Attribution:* Study cross-channel results and spend and CPAs by channel and program; model comparisons by channel.
- *Scenario planning:* Run what-if scenarios that leverage the cross-channel interplay from attribution models.
- *Optimization:* Make audience, media, and channel optimization changes to maximize program performance.

THE HEART OF THE MATTER

The fundamentals of execution are at the heart of this chapter. Following are the main points to remember:

- The foundational capability for success in any CRM platform is connected data. The ability to collect, cleanse, and associate all data into a holistic consumer view is key. This includes rationalizing known and anonymous data together as well as interactive (online) and noninteractive (offline) data. This approach sets the stage for a longitudinal view of consumer interactions, which is used to drive relevant, insight-driven CRM execution.
- The enabling infrastructure and supporting processes require that analytics be embedded into the solution itself, as opposed to conducting analytics in isolation. The insights platform

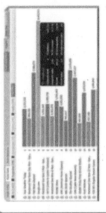

Customer Segmentation

Optimization

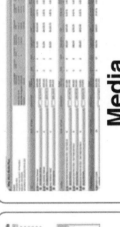

Media Targeting

Scenario Planning

Dashboard

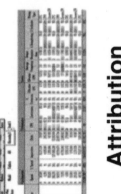

Attribution

FIGURE 8.4 User Access Console

component is dedicated to supporting analytics and operation-alizing frameworks and metrics to drive insight-driven CRM execution. These frameworks include sophisticated attribution modeling that uses the compiled event stream, actionable metrics that trigger appropriate communications proactively, and data constructs that provide ready access to insight for putting CRM strategies into action. This approach makes analytics a core driver of CRM execution. Data is arranged such that insights are readily available and actionable.

- A centralized decision management hub is needed to manage consumer interactions. This approach guards against uncoordinated decisions in isolation, which can lead to broken consumer experiences and frustration. This component includes a rules engine, an open omni-channel connectivity mechanism, testing and machine learning capability, and the ability to support interactions in real time. The end result is coordinated consumer communications from the brand, one voice, an enterprise-wide approach to CRM to drive relevant communications, and more value being driven with every consumer interaction.

Chapter 9 Organization and Leadership

Permission Is Not Sponsorship

When many companies think about customer relationship marketing (CRM), they seldom fully consider the organizational implications: getting leaders aligned behind CRM, getting work groups to work together, identifying job design and skills, defining organizational processes, and creating incentives. The organization component of Connected CRM (cCRM) is the enabler that aligns the company to the customer vision and ensures cCRM functions are performed across the enterprise. Organization is the most misunderstood and underappreciated aspect of CRM. It's difficult to quantify and goes hand in hand with the taboo subject of change.

There isn't a big organization database to build. There isn't a downloadable organization app; there's no standard blueprint. Companies aren't really ever sure they're doing it right. And let's face it, organizational discussions are uncomfortable. Yet, deep down, we all know they're important.

Here's why: Organization is the secret sauce for CRM success. If you're adopting a cCRM approach, it's really the

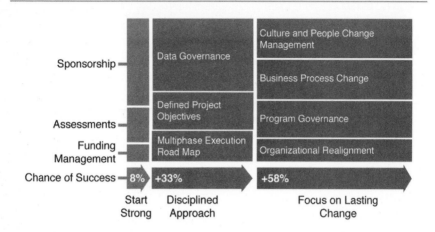

Study of nearly 400 business leaders worldwide, Success drivers explained 65 percent. Low percentage indicates activities common to high and low performers. High percentage indicates activities more unique to top performers.

FIGURE 9.1   How Top Organizations Make CRM Stick

Source: http://www-935.ibm.com/services/uk/gbs/pdf/Breaking_away_with_business_analytics_and_optimisation.pdf

organizational elements—as much as the infrastructure—that make the difference between success and failure. Research done several years ago identified that sponsorship, assessments, and funding, although critical, will get you only 8 percent of the way there (see Figure 9.1). Adding to it a disciplined approach to data and projects—the expensive stuff—will get you to the 40 percent mark.[1] Basically, that translates into success two out of every five times.[2] Those are weak odds considering the investment! It's not until you tackle organization—issues such as culture, change management, process, governance, and alignment—that the odds become favorable. They don't cost a lot of money but require thoughtful attention. Ironically, we do the expensive stuff that's relatively easy, but we don't do the inexpensive stuff that's difficult.

My team has identified six key organizational building blocks that are most critical for CRM success:

- *Business strategy alignment:* ensuring that your CRM strategy aligns with your overall business strategies and goals
- *Leadership alignment:* capturing and sustaining executive support
- *Integrated structure:* determining who does what at every level
- *Job design and skills:* defining key roles and who has decision-making authority
- *Linked interactions and processes:* establishing handoffs and business rules
- *Complementary incentives:* driving performance using the right success metrics

BUSINESS STRATEGY ALIGNMENT

Successful CRM efforts start with a clear understanding of business strategies and goals; this is particularly the case with major CRM transformation efforts. CRM must reflect overall business objectives and be in sync with them, not competing with them.

A classic example is a situation in which a company's overall business strategy is focused on customer acquisition, but the CRM efforts are primarily geared around retention and/or cross-selling. A more subtle example is when the overall business strategy calls for specific engagement strategies by defined customer segments, but many CRM touchpoints are driven not by segment strategy but by CRM analytics that do not reflect those segment strategies, such as analysis of customer profitability and/or direct marketing responsiveness.

Decisions regarding CRM investments also need to reflect overall business strategies. Where should a company invest in CRM technology and other CRM capabilities? How does a company sort out and prioritize the various requests for investment? You must have a defined methodology, based in part on business strategy and in part on how those investments will drive specific business results, to prioritize such investments.

LEADERSHIP ALIGNMENT

The most critical element for leadership alignment is clear and enthusiastic executive commitment and sponsorship. What does it mean in your organization to be an executive sponsor? What are the inflection points when executive sponsorship matters most?

Sponsorship is more than just lip service; executive sponsors must be prepared to publicly assert their support *and* put their personal credibility at stake. They must display genuine interest and devote time and energy demonstrating their support. Organizations "snap to" leadership direction; in its absence, the organization will simply not see your CRM efforts as a priority.

Are you really committed to doing things differently? Do you have the stomach to drive the necessary organizational transformation? Executive permission is not sponsorship, and permission alone will not enable the organization to break through all of its institutional barriers to change. Permission may work in levels 1 to 3 of the CRM maturity continuum, but it will not be sufficient to break through the glass ceiling into true cCRM.

Leadership alignment also requires clear understanding and buy-in to a well-articulated CRM vision—how the organization will understand and consistently engage its customers. Do you have a CRM vision, and supporting CRM strategy, that is clearly articulated and effectively communicated to your leadership across the organization? Is the CRM vision realistic based on your business model? Is it actionable? Do your executives both understand and buy into the CRM vision? If not, why not? Are incentives and metrics in place for a sense of shared success and failure, or are you stuck in the paradigm where some executives believe that their end of the boat does not have any holes? Have you translated the CRM vision and strategy to each business unit and channel so that each part of the organization knows how it is affected?

With executive sponsorship comes financial commitment—the willingness to provide the necessary investments in a cCRM infrastructure and other capabilities. Money makes it happen. Far too many companies have asserted their intent to become customer centric without providing sufficient funding for the various CRM initiatives required to achieve that. Financial commitment forces executives to get engaged. And a business case that supports financial commitment by clearly identifying the benefits and costs of the CRM/customer effort over time is a critical requirement to secure financial commitment.

It may be helpful to think of the business case as a change management tool. It frames the discussion around value to the organization. Buy-in for the business case across executive leadership ranks is critical. The true value of the business case is the fact that it is widely accepted by the organization. It represents a commitment; otherwise, it doesn't mean anything. It also provides direction to the different parts of the organization, to identify which groups are responsible for achieving *this* or *that* revenue goal and which groups are responsible for bringing CRM initiatives to life at *that* cost.

The business case can further help identify the scale of the cCRM opportunity. What's the potential return compared against the required cost? Is a major transformational CRM effort justified? If you can't identify sufficient revenue improvements or cost reductions to justify the required investment, it may be time to take a second look at the scale of investment to be made.

A related factor is whether the upside benefits are material; will the potential return be meaningful for your organization? A projected 5-year return of $50 million may be significant for a midsized organization but relatively trivial for a $20 billion enterprise and hardly worth the organizational pivot required to achieve it, especially relative to other opportunities.

INTEGRATED STRUCTURE

Another key organizational building block to cCRM is the ability to execute in an integrated way across the entire

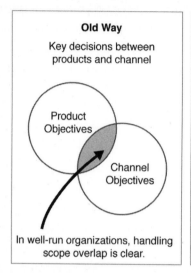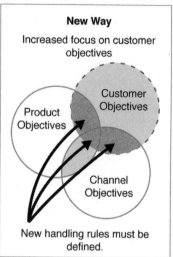

FIGURE 9.2 Governance in a cCRM World

organization. In most companies it used to be that key decisions were made based on product and channel and handling the overlap between the two was fairly clear. As previous chapters have stressed, many companies today are placing increased focus on customer objectives. The challenge is that customer objectives tend to greatly overlap with *both* product objectives and channel objectives, which can lead to fairly significant challenges between those work groups. New rules must be defined to handle these points of overlap (Figure 9.2).

Decision making—governance—in organizations that are organized by product is relatively easy; the lines of responsibility are generally pretty clear cut. But decision making in a matrixed organization, such as an organization that has introduced customer segment managers, is much harder. It's often not clear in such organizations who has the authority to make decisions. And without clear decision-making authority, organizations can quickly devolve into a culture of turf wars and end-around maneuvers.

Overlapping decision hierarchies, unaligned decision makers, and conflicting incentives are a recipe for waste, poor results, and behaviors unhealthy to the overall organization. Ambiguous decision authority can thwart strategic initiatives and impede necessary change. The net result is that cCRM transformation is unlikely to stick.

So how do you fix this? First, agree on rules and operating guidelines before you get into specific situations. Second, set up a decision hierarchy that clearly establishes who gets to decide what. The roles that previously made decisions in a product- and channel-focused company may no longer be the best roles to make those decisions in a new model. Third, figure out who is accountable—and therefore has the decision-making role—and who is in an advisory, influencing role. Fourth, determine the latitude that each person has to make decisions that impact other work groups. And fifth, set up formal mechanisms to resolve and mediate the inevitable disputes.

Clearly defining roles and responsibilities is critical. Many companies have successfully deployed the RACI model: who is *responsible*, who is *accountable*, who is *consulted*, and who is *informed*. The "responsible" tag is given to the person or persons assigned to do the work; note that responsibility can be shared. The "accountable" tag is given to the person who makes the final decision and has the ultimate ownership; there is only one accountable person in a given situation. Being account-able means having yes/no authority and the power to veto. The "consulted" tag is given to the person or persons who *must* be consulted before a decision or action is taken; this person or persons are likely subject matter experts (SMEs). Two-way dialog is critical when engaging a consulted person. The "informed" tag is assigned to those who must be informed that a decision or action has been taken; this is typically a one-way dialog.

The RACI model can be used to define the span of authority, set expectations, define roles and work groups, identify required skills, manage performance, and define hiring and training needs. The RACI model can be successfully deployed across multiple levels of the organization: executive leadership, with a particular focus on major decision making; work groups, to help set brighter lines about scope of responsibility and control; and individual roles. Clarity is needed at all levels.

A good illustration of a very common integration challenge in most CRM-focused organizations is figuring out the right place for the customer analytics function. Should analytics be organized within each line of business? Should analytics be in a centralized corporate group? A research study published in the MIT Sloan Management Review in 2010 found that when most companies initially realize their need for analytics, they turn first to resources within a business unit, not a centralized analytics group.[3] Over time, centralized analytic groups emerge that can bring a shared enterprise perspective and also deploy more sophisticated tools. Typically, though, these centralized analytic groups are *in addition* to local business unit analytic resources.

JOB DESIGN AND SKILLS

Another core organizational success driver for cCRM is getting the appropriate human resources with the right attributes and training in place and ensuring that they have clearly defined roles, responsibilities, and accountabilities. This potentially means considering new roles in your organization.

Recent research conducted by Merkle on customer-centric transformation identified that there is a clear correlation between organizations with "top talent" and overall company performance. Our research found that top growth companies are most mature in CRM. Those organizations are more customer oriented, with deeper customer understanding and a greater ability to customize and personalize customer interactions. They also put a greater effort into understanding the effect of their marketing activities. These organizations are routinely able to:

- Manage a comprehensive view of customers.
- Understand, identify, segment, and manage customers based on their value.
- Allocate resources to optimize long-term customer value.
- Customize and personalize customer interactions.
- Understand the incremental impact of each marketing activity.
- Respond to changes in customer, competitor, and marketplace conditions faster than competitors.

What are the key *attributes* of top talent? How do you know when you have it? The short answer is that it requires both the right people, with the right attributes, and the right organizational culture. It requires employees—and a supportive company culture—who are collaborative, decisive, and proactive.

Top growth companies that are most mature in CRM report that their organization and people are routinely able to:

- Collaborate with employees outside of their department for the benefit of customers.
- Analyze, decide, and act upon decisions related to customers.
- Use the same customer value metrics consistently across the organization.
- Challenge the status quo to create new opportunities and business outcomes.
- Predict and prepare for the future by proactively evaluating trade-offs.

Over the past decade, we've seen the emergence of new roles to reflect the greater organizational focus on CRM. One of the most common is the chief customer officer, also known in some companies as the chief experience officer or chief client officer. Forrester has written about the increase in the number of companies that have a single executive leading customer experience efforts across a business unit or an entire company.[4] Call them what you will, CCO or CXO, they are often on the executive management team within a company, which means they have influence over how the company manages CRM and customer engagement. They are often prime motivators of CRM change, especially in highly regulated industries such as financial services, telecommunications, and health care, as well as in the software industry.

Why are they important? They can play a significant role in driving customer experience. Forrester has identified three ways that they can make big customer experience improvements that lead to profits:

- Create end-to-end accountability for the customer experience
- Focus on design experiences rather than processes
- Shift culture, especially as they move from advisory-type roles to more operationally structured roles

Forrester cautioned that the CCO/CXO role is not a "silver bullet" for a company's customer experience problems and that the role should be created only if there is a strategic mandate, cultural maturity, and if the role has the "clout and tools to change the way a firm operates."[5]

A second interesting emerging role is that of the marketing technology officer (MTO). The emergence of the MTO reflects the fact that marketing, and especially what used to be called below-the-line marketing (now more commonly called CRM), is increasingly enabled by technology: data, database management, analytics, digital, and marketing communications. The lines between the marketing and IT departments are increasingly blurring.

As the chief technology officer (CTO) of Ion Interactive has said, "The challenge isn't making the technology work; it's having marketing embed an understanding of technology into its creative and strategic mission. The more distance between IT and marketing, the more you miss opportunities."[6] This may take several forms: (1) a marketing-focused team within IT,

(2) creation of a marketing technology group within marketing, or (3) a coordination role between marketing and IT to coordinate activities. Forrester has called the goal of the MTO to act as an "internal startup," because they break through existing silos in marketing and IT and get past turf wars, bottlenecks, and inflexibility. They can more nimbly develop and scale emerging capabilities. They can centralize resources, such as user experience designers and marketing scientists, with the goal of eventually reaching scale across the enterprise. And they can effectively partner with IT and other internal groups, positioned as they are with close ties to both the chief marketing officer (CMO) and the chief information officer (CIO).

Forrester goes on to identify seven major responsibilities for the MTO[7]:

1. Sets marketing technology strategy
2. Develops marketing applications
3. Captures and integrates customer data
4. Measures the performance and return of marketing technology
5. Drafts technology requirements and conducts vendor selection
6. Conducts audits of customer data and marketing applications
7. Manages technology vendors and partners

The third emerging role, the platform marketer, is driven by digital media achieving addressability at scale. For example, Facebook, Google, and Twitter can now target enough specific individuals to make them viable audience platforms for one-to-one marketing. This platform marketer will have the forethought to understand how to create value for the organization through the inherent addressability of the digital platforms. They will work their way backward from the desired end state, collaborating with other parts of the organization.

The platform marketer will be a powerful agent of change inside these organizations, wearing many hats and embodying the collective competencies needed to successfully operate in this world of addressability at scale.

1. Marketing technologist and audience platform expert
2. Programmatic media buyer and addressability expert
3. Customer experience designer
4. Consumer privacy and preference advocate
5. Decision science, measurement, and attribution expert
6. Multi-channel program strategist
7. Segment portfolio manager

Obviously, these three emerging marketing roles, the CCO/CXO, the MTO, and the platform marketer, would be virtually impossible to fill with one individual. The idea is that marketing teams need to evolve to fit the bill, meeting the demands of today's big-data-driven, digitally enabled customer engagements.

LINKED INTERACTIONS AND PROCESSES

Business units and other work groups are logically focused on their own business objectives, and pursuit of those objectives often leads to conflicts with other work groups. It's natural that business work groups will tend to pursue their own objectives, even if those objectives are inadvertently at odds with the objectives of other groups. One of greatest challenges with reducing those work group conflicts is breaking down internal silos, which means defined processes and effective handoffs, information handling between work groups, and common business rules.

Defined processes and accountabilities go hand in hand. It is critical to understand and articulate exactly who in the organization is responsible for which processes, especially customer-facing processes. USAA, the Texas-based financial services and insurance company in San Antonio, Texas, recognized the need to clearly defined internal ownership for the processes that support the USAA customer experience. Already well known for its member service, USAA management looked for further ways to enhance what they call the "member experience," especially the goal of providing customers with an integrated set of services using a wide-ranging set of technologies. To do so, USAA identified approximately 100 key experiences associated with customer journeys (for example, buying a car or deploying abroad) and then designated owners and/or cross-functional teams for each experience. The owners and teams were then held accountable for the processes that support those customer journey experiences.[8]

What are the process improvement steps that you have taken to deploy CRM in *your* organization? Are your process improvement efforts narrowly focused within business silos, or do they span work groups? Do they span marketing, sales, and service? What is your approach to identifying the necessary process improvements? Many customer experience leaders recognize that pushing change across an organization is difficult and turn to business process improvement teams for help. A true organizational transformation requires changing the beliefs and behavioral norms of everyone in the company, and customer experience leaders can't do this alone. It's one thing to define ideal business processes; it's another to get the organization to adopt them.

Some companies recognize the need to drive internal change and identify people who can serve as change agents. One example is Intuit, which has 200 "innovation catalysts" who are specially trained to identify innovation opportunities, including process improvements, across the Intuit organization.

The CRM marketplace has responded to the need for coordination between work groups with the development of automation software, including marketing resource management (MRM) tools. These software tools are designed to enhance a company's ability to orchestrate and optimize internal and external marketing resources. MRM applications enable companies to:

- Plan and budget for marketing activities and programs (strategic planning and financial management).
- Create and develop marketing programs and content (creative product management).
- Collect and manage content and knowledge (digital asset, content, and knowledge management).
- Fulfill and distribute marketing assets, content, and collateral (marketing fulfillment).
- Measure, analyze, and optimize marketing performance (MRM analytics).

These tools essentially put in place a workflow that allows for efficient management of campaign-level marketing review and approval processes. They're extremely helpful for managing those processes across work groups within a company and for processes that span a company and its agency partners.

A critical success factor is defining and communicating a common set of business rules across the organization. One example is customer preferences; surprisingly, many companies have not yet developed a common approach to customer preferences such as opt-ins, opt-outs, and so on. For example, a customer may express a telephone opt-out preference to one business unit and be surprised (read: annoyed) to continue to receive telephone solicitations from another business unit in the same company. For a company with business units engaging their customers across multiple channels, this can be surprisingly challenging, yet critical for customer satisfaction.

Another related example is pricing across channels. A major bookseller today offers an attractive online price for books sold through that channel and even offers to allow customers to pick up their purchases at a local store, only to surprise them with a higher price point for books picked up in the store.

One area where linked interactions and processes are particularly important is on the front lines of customer engagement, whether that be retail store associates, customer service representatives in a contact center, front desk staff at hotels, or your sales team. Empowering your frontline personnel is critical. It is truly the last mile of cCRM, and those customer interactions typically represent critical moments for winning the customer relationship—and the key factor in determining whether cCRM investments are successful.

We've identified several key factors for frontline empowerment. First, establish and communicate clear values, service standards, and the right organizational attitude that reflects your brand. Second, where possible, leverage technology, including technologies to direct employees, capture customer feedback from digital sources, and respond quickly. Third, think globally and act locally: Equip the front line with the ability to meet local market and customer needs, including localized marketing tools and processes if appropriate.

The ability of organizations to empower frontline personnel to achieve cCRM goals depends to a great extent on the business model. A highly centralized, command-and-control organization with strict standard operating procedures (SOPs) is not likely to be able to execute empowered frontline CRM as well as other companies. Take, for example, McDonald's. McDonald's and similar organizations teach operational standards and tactics and succeed on the basis of their operational standardization and related efficiency.

Other organizations that are oriented more toward values and attitudes than operational efficiency are far more likely to be successful with cCRM. For example, luxury hoteliers (such as Four Seasons) and upscale clothing retailers (such as Nordstrom or Neiman Marcus) teach values and focus on communicating the right attitudes for their associates to adopt. They strive to teach service standards and values and then empower their people to act on those values. Typically, these organizations are more decentralized, with operating elements that are largely independent (individual hotels, individual stores).

The latter model focusing on values and attitude is more consistent with customer expectations. Customers want choice and have increased expectations for the customer experience.

Differentiating frontline customer engagement is also critical but can be challenging given employee turnover in frontline roles. The key is to fully understand customer segments and then simplify the communication to frontline personnel of those customer segments and how they should be treated. Many airlines, hotel operators, retailers, and other industries effectively leverage loyalty program tiers to achieve this goal. For example, front desk personnel at many hotels know *exactly* how to engage a customer based on their status within the loyalty program and reward higher-status guests with room upgrades, amenities, late checkouts, and more.

Merkle recently helped a life insurance company define the right customer engagement strategy for its customer segments by using workshops and other facilitation techniques; then an internal communications campaign and training were developed to educate the organization, including the call center, on each segment and how each segment should be engaged.

Marketing is increasingly local, especially given available technology. Empowering the person in an organization who is closest to the customer can be a substantial advantage. This is especially powerful if an organization can combine customer data with insightful analytics and provide the frontline personnel with the right customer treatment based on those analytics. It can be even more powerful if the organization has a culture that empowers employees to act.

The evolution of technology has also allowed frontline personnel to be less focused on the transaction itself and more focused on customer engagement. Modern point-of-sale (POS) systems simplify the purchase process, and many POS systems can relay key information about the customer, if available. In such cases, frontline employees' time can be used to engage the customer with purchase recommendations (suggested selling). For example, shoe retailers may identify the segments value seekers and family buyers; the store associate can be trained to recommend special offers to value seekers or can recommend specific shoe styles for the family buyers.

Empowering frontline staff is particularly applicable to high-involvement categories. Take, for example, a retail dealership for snowmobiles and ATVs. How can the manufacturer of a line of snowmobiles empower the dealer while maintaining brand standards? Manufacturers are providing dealers with branded, multi-channel promotional collateral along with the capability to customize the promotional template with their own indicia and offers. Also known as distributed marketing or localized marketing, this enables corporate marketers to maintain brand standards and enables local marketers to respond quickly to local-level market conditions. Customer data and insightful analytics can further boost the power of the message with specific targeting to the right audience in the right channel.

COMPLEMENTARY INCENTIVES

Shared metrics, or currencies, are also critical for integrated work groups toward a common CRM goal. As described in earlier chapters, Merkle has identified three currencies that are critical for integration across your organization:

- Segmentation currency
- Customer value currency
- Measurement currency

Every company segments its customers in one way or another, whether it be customer value segments, products or channels used, attitudinal segmentation, or countless other segmentation approaches. Having multiple segments is okay; in fact, it's kind of the point. Each segmentation approach provides insight into customers, their value, their needs, and their behavior. But it's critical to deploy a single segmentation approach when engaging customers, especially in customer service engagement. A single segmentation approach—currency—allows the organization to rally around a common understanding of customers and engage with each customer segment in a consistent and logical way.

DirecTV, a Merkle client, uses a customer value currency called the Heart Program. Each customer is assessed based on his or her value and assigned a Heart Score from 1 to 5. The more hearts, the more valuable the customer and the better the customer treatment. Customers with the highest anticipated lifetime value to the company are labeled 5-heart customers. They are loyal to DirecTV, have excellent credit, and pay their bills on time. They subscribe to premium packages and order additional services, such as pay-per-view events and movies. At the other end of the scale are those customers who switch from service to service in search of a better deal. These customers could actually end up costing DirecTV money, given the investment DirecTV makes in hardware, installation, and marketing to set up a new subscriber.

Most important, the Heart Score provides a relatively simple mechanism to communicate across the organization, especially the customer contact center, and drives consistent customer treatment. For example, customer service representatives (CSRs) are now empowered to engage customers with the right offers and service recovery options based on their value to DirecTV.

Metrics must also be aligned across business groups. A classic case is misalignment between metrics that measure a call center on average handle time—basically getting the customer off the phone as quickly as possible—and other metrics in the same organization that measure customer satisfaction with customer service. Clearly, these two sets of metrics are not aligned and can be diametrically opposed to each other.

Another example is a bank that incents its various channels based on completed new account applications; they found that customers who started an application online and then went into a branch for assistance to complete the application were forced to start the application process all over again, because the branch gets credit only for applications they initiate and complete! Taking this approach is great for the branch's metrics but a real pain in the neck for the customer.

THE HEART OF THE MATTER

Following are some the main points to remember from this chapter:

- Organizational issues and resistance are often-cursed by-products of CRM—neglected and often mistreated—yet the organization is arguably one of the most important factors to address for CRM success.
- Without leadership alignment, clear roles and responsibilities, defined decision authority, the right success metrics, and so forth, CRM is difficult to implement and execute. It can be uncomfortable to tackle these issues, and the organization may resist, especially when roles are redefined and responsibilities are modified.
- Addressing the organizational aspects of CRM change takes time; there's no quick fix. However, it can go a long way toward maximizing your CRM investments.

Three

WHAT'S NEXT?

Chapter 10 Making It Happen

Realizing Your Customer-Centric Transformation

Merkle completed a study in 2013 to investigate how large U.S. organizations drive value using customer relationship marketing (CRM).[1] The study looked at overall perceptions of CRM and explored factors that are correlated with successful execution. We presented more than 350 executive-level respondents across multiple industries with 18 different CRM success drivers and asked them to cite to what extent they performed or pursued the particular success driver. We then isolated the win-win, the group where organizational success and individual success occurred, and the lose-lose, the group where organizational success and individual success did not occur, to understand what worked and what didn't. We were intrigued by the insight that leaders often aren't successful, even if the initiative is regarded as successful in the organization. Conversely, leaders sometimes find success even without effective execution of a CRM strategy. Conflicting incentives negatively affect success rates.

The 18 success drivers gave us the basis to identify five areas that are key to successful CRM change. These keys are designed to create the focus needed to align leadership and organizational success. They represent both the greatest struggles and the most promising opportunities for organizations. Although they are not an exhaustive catalog of every change practice, they are essential areas that represent both the greatest struggles and most promising opportunities for organizations.

- *Key 1: Sponsorship:* Effort and commitment matter significantly. Permission does not equal sponsorship. An executive mandate is the only way to achieve success.
- *Key 2: Customer vision:* Open communication brings the customer vision to life, makes it easy for people to understand at all levels, and sets the stage for the operating changes to come.
- *Key 3: Target operating approach:* Leaders across the enterprise need to accept the fact that their roles and organizations will have to adjust and gain clarity on the changes in day-to-day activities.
- *Key 4: Planning and financial commitments:* Stakeholders must commit to the plan and to following through. Establish timelines, expectations, and financial results metrics.
- *Key 5: Implementation and change management:* You must find effective ways to sustain broad support through the difficult periods and continuously prove the value along the way.

In aggregate, we found that the win-win respondents used the CRM change success factors 65 percent of the time, or nearly three times more than the lose-lose group, who utilized them only 26 percent of the time. The lose-lose struggled to get to average, whereas the win-win group used better-than-average effort more than 80 percent of the time.

KEY 1: SPONSORSHIP—CHAMPION THE CAUSE

Sponsorship and leadership alignment is where the win-win organizations excel—and where the lose-lose organizations could be setting themselves up for failure. In our research, the win-win group performed these three leadership activities to a much larger degree than the lose-lose group:

• Clear and persistent executive-level sponsorship
• Focus on a major, high-profile business need
• Executive leadership steering committee guidance

The most important drivers for gaining sponsorship are materiality and engagement. If the value is small or the change is not big enough or meaningful enough to the organization, it's not going to be important to the top executives either. In addition, good leaders delegate for sure, but they must remain actively and energetically committed to and engaged in the project to achieve alignment and ensure its success.

The opportunity must be significant enough in its scale, and especially business impact (for example, "This change will move our stock price"), to garner the support and engagement of the senior leaders. CRM is not a database, an application, a campaign, or some other similar tactic. Should a chief executive officer (CEO) be daily engaged in a data warehouse project? Probably not.

The change must be presented with a broad-facing and fundamental business impact that will change how the organization interacts with or delivers for customers. The CRM change will be stated in terms that describe persuasive and meaningful business transformation, such as, "We are going to become our customers' most trusted financial advisors" or "We are going to apply customer insight into every customer interaction."

The benefits need to be clear and quantifiable, either to solve an issue that is limiting growth or to capitalize on a new insight to leapfrog competitors. This is vastly different from testing a new marketing program, buying a campaign management tool, or building some reports.

Perhaps more genuine indicators of materiality are whether the change moves the organization's marketplace pricing power; whether it severely disrupts the competitor set; whether it fundamentally transforms how customers interact; whether it has a sea-change effect in revenue, margin, or stock price; or whether it requires large populations of managers and employees to do things differently.

At the least, the scale must be enough to capture attention. In much the same way that price signals quality, the level of investment, or crudely the price tag, is likely an indicator of materiality. Is a million-dollar project going to move a multibillion-dollar organization? Doubtful. Keep in mind that an initially low price tag may simply be the ante, or even wishful thinking.

Does this feel familiar at all? A unit or functional leader makes a pitch to the CEO or other senior executive for a CRM change. The CEO gladly agrees: "Sure, report back to me when it is done and let me know how it went."

Fail.

Permission is simply not sponsorship. Permission is passive, unengaged, and sometimes even dismissive. Sponsorship is active, engaged, supportive, and enthusiastic. Most important, it supports alignment, meaning it steers the individuals who must work together to do so in ways that drive the core organizational objectives while also enabling these people to succeed individually. The team driving day-to-day performance is responsible for success, but accountability lies squarely with the sponsor, whether it's the CEO or a direct report. Levels below this can sponsor change but of a much narrower scale and probably contained within the personal scope of their role.

What does good sponsorship look like?

The Sponsoring Executive:

- Assumes accountability for the initiative, taking pride in its successes and owning up to its failures.

- Requires updates from the team leaders frequently and reviews them with genuine interest and urgency.
- Asks about how it is going, not only from people working on the initiative, but also from people who are affected by it.
- Readily sets priorities and clears away distractions. This requires understanding the entire project portfolio and ensuring that people stay focused on the main goal, versus the pet projects that distract from the big win.
- Makes it a mandate, and, if smart, doesn't make everything and all minutiae a mandate all the time.
- Keeps his or her advocacy for the project a public and visible act for the organization to see.
- Makes sure the initiative stays on the agenda.

Counter this with initiatives that have inadequate sponsorship or mere permission.

The Executive Who Gave Inadequate Support or Permission Only:

- Simply writes the check.
- Joins the kickoff and then just listens in for quarterly updates.
- Neither celebrates its success nor laments its failure.
- Doesn't work to clear distractions, solve disputes, or make decisions.
- Doesn't insist that the organization actively engage in the change, permitting employees to opt out.

One executive responded with a story about his CEO, who told the respondent that he would be "the decisive change agent for CRM within the organization." The executive then went to task building a transformative program, planning fundamental changes that would truly transform the organization toward a customer-centric business model. When he finally released his plans and insisted that the groups begin the transformation, he was largely ignored. The CEO's instruction resembled nothing like sponsorship; in fact, the executive had no support at all. He disappointedly moved on from the organization, having spent a fruitless year of hard work to ultimately accomplish nothing.

KEY 2: CUSTOMER VISION—SHOWCASE THE NEW CUSTOMER EXPERIENCE

Our experience shows us that it's easier to talk about the need for change in others than the need for change in ourselves. By separating how insight enables better customer experiences from how it is actually done, we minimize objections that are more rooted in a fear of changing day-to-day activities or management authorities. Because typically no single group owns the customer experience, the showcase allows team members and managers to see how the proposed changes would bring more value to the customer and thus more value to the organization when adopted.

To convince the broader population—and often key leaders—of the value of CRM, it is vital to showcase (versus "use case") how interactions with customers need to change and why it's valuable. Building the customer experience is often done from the outside in, meaning that you imagine what the customer experiences with the organization are like from the customer's point of view. The experiences are meant to drive satisfaction, increase ease of purchasing, entice more spending, build loyalty and advocacy, make new sales, change customer behavior, and so forth.

Customer interaction needs to transcend an intellectual or analytical conversation and become an emotional one. Few people have made a persuasive case using a process swimlane chart, where one customer-facing function works totally separate from another. Frankly, they're boring and dismissible and communicate little about what the customer will experience. Your showcase team needs a combination of business acumen, analytics, and creative talent, all acting in a consultative fashion to the organization.

Although the showcase is an excellent way to communicate and drive excitement, it is dependent upon rigorous business analysis. This analysis should be based in large part on how to enhance customer engagement, at both the segment and individual level, with better insight. Without such analysis, it runs the risk of being viewed as a fluff piece, a clever narrative that doesn't do much and brings little or no value.

In practice, the showcase should be based on customer experience design tools that also support business requirements. If it fails to do this, extra steps will be needed, and the excitement from the showcase can diminish as a secondary requirements exercise is completed. There's a large portfolio of analysis and planning techniques that are associated with customer experience design, and all of them have specific value. Some of them include:

- Use cases
- Customer experience workshops, secondary analysis, and primary research
- Customer interaction and journey mapping
- Moment-of-truth and point-of-pain analysis

All these techniques have proven value and typically require experienced specialists to perform them properly and ensure that they have the intended organizational and downstream effects.

It's important to generate excitement and advocacy, and a showcase is a terrific way to do so. A great showcase is typically manifested in a creative project that viscerally shows what the new customer experience will be while also highlighting what's not working. It won't necessarily show the entire experience or be representative of everything that will change, but it will find a key pivotal moment that clearly shows how the transformation will affect daily business. It is a tool to build clarity, excitement, advocacy, and understanding. The showcase helps create a rallying cry for the change. Showcase formats could include:

- Videos of customer experiences, complete with acted-out scenarios and real-life situations
- Visual displays that might show key interaction points, such as sample campaign collateral or interaction scripts
- Comic strips or "day in the life" renderings showing customers acting in their environment
- Pilots and demos with hands-on experiences

One insurer built an internal interactive campaign for front-line professionals that showed how different customer segments had different needs. It highlighted how personalizing the customer experience, if only at the segment level, would transform the customer experience to increase close rates as they launched their new direct-to-consumer business. Every employee participated and received informative takeaway collateral that became a real symbol that things were changing and a persistent reminder of how they needed to behave differently.

A health plan company had a mess of an onboarding process that involved countless pages of dry, often repetitive forms, with policy details that drove customers either to feeling frustration or apathy toward the organization. The future customer experience for joining would be crisp, lively, and easy. The organization set up a customer experience showcase that featured exhibits of both the bad experiences and the new improved ones. One exhibit was the "pit of paper" showing a waterfall of old forms spewing into a desperate pit of paperwork!

Showcases highlight negative examples, too. One clever team from a telecommunications company mystery shopped through its call center and a competitor's to show differences in the customer experience. They produced a video of a bad sales call that took many transfers, multiple hold times, and 45 minutes of pain-inducing reality as the customer was routinely sent from agent to agent and then placed back on hold. In contrast, their competitors were able to quickly and efficiently handle the same set of inquires 80 percent faster. When the executives were shown their own dismal sales experience, they slunk down in their chairs, embarrassed. Of course, this became a powerful rallying point; they instantly agreed that change was needed and committed to a new path. Resistance simply melted away.

KEY 3: TARGET OPERATING APPROACH—COME TO TERMS (WITH CHANGE AND YOUR COHORTS)

By *coming to terms* we mean two things. First, it is simply about accepting that things are going to be different, and people will need to adapt for continued success. Second, and perhaps even more challenging, it is about negotiating changes to the span of authority and incentives tied to performance.

The main point here, beyond the design, is to send the message to employees that the change is really going to happen and to make it 100 percent clear that they cannot avoid it. This can be excruciating for many, especially if they've been successful doing something one way for a long time.

In our research, the win-win group actively pursued these many design and capability planning activities to a larger degree than the lose-lose group, including adjustments to incentives and metrics; changes to work groups or organizational structure (such as segment managers); updated business processes, including training and/or automation; deployment of new applications (such as campaign management, analytics); enhancements to existing applications (such as channel systems); objective assessment and benchmarking; and new or expanded data capabilities.

This phase is about clarity rather than the certainty of minutia. Clarity drives progress, whereas certainty is a tollgate and is virtually unattainable in complex ecosystems. It's about understanding new target architectures—solution, data, process, organization, and more. Early on, you don't need to be focused on generating detailed business and system requirements. Instead, you should use the business analysis supporting your showcase to frame a big-picture view of how the major activities need to come together. It helps to have a leading practice reference model such as Connected CRM to ensure you cover all the required parts of the new operating approach. For example, it includes:

- Enterprise segmentation that supports customer strategy and forms the basis for planning based on customer value metrics
- A strong financial management competency that utilizes measurement and attribution techniques to enable media and channel budget application
- An integrated targeting and customization competency that supports media and channel planning for personalized experience delivery
- Infrastructure and processes that enable an enterprise CRM approach that encompasses the data, systems, tools, and technologies required for ongoing management and execution
- An organization that spans leadership and management decision rights, work groups and how they collaborate, and empowered top talent with the right incentives.

Determining what the organization has to add or change must align with the unchallenged agreement that comes out of designing the new operating approach. This is where the key actors in the change must come to terms with the fact that the change is real. It is part design and part consensus building. For example, an activity previously done by the channel team might now be done by a segment management group. New reporting structures might be introduced. Profit and loss (P&L) responsibility may shift. Day-to-day work might be automated. Accountabilities may move among marketing, sales, service, product, segment managers, or channel/media owners.

If your vision is about technology or data only, it's incomplete and risky. More than 60 percent of winners put a lot of effort into these activities across the board. It's hard work, but it's easier to do before you're in the middle of a change program or dealing with a solution in the process of being rejected by the organization. It's okay if some topics are uncomfortable. But if you're avoiding a topic, you have a problem. You need to expose any breakdowns in alignment on the vision and underlying hidden assumptions.

It's important to assign decision rights. Although not all do, many large organizations employ a matrix-based management approach. Matrices balance multiple, ideally complementary objectives by allocating decision rights throughout the organization. Most organizations have well-entrenched ways of viewing their business with executive and individual performance incentives tied to their results. In a matrix model, organizations must decide what role customer centricity plays in how they run their businesses. Essentially, where does customer centricity fall in the decision-making hierarchy, and who gets to decide what? Do channel teams become service providers to segment teams? Do segment teams merely advise channel teams on how to refine their approach? Financially, who owns the P&L? Who is a cost center?

How leadership reallocates decision rights and performance incentives to fit the new operating approach will be one of your biggest challenges and possibly a source of unwanted drama. Understand that business as usual eats change for lunch when there isn't clarity and alignment in the operating approach. Leaders need to help others see how they can succeed and grow under the new model. As we noted earlier, this part is going to be a negotiation to come to terms, especially with the more senior executives.

KEY 4: PLANNING AND FINANCIAL COMMITMENTS— COMMIT TO THE PLAN

This key applies more at the executive leadership and senior management levels in the organization. The heart of the matter is that the people in the organization need to agree to deliver new customer experiences, accept how the organization needs to be aligned, and then do something about it. We've all been in meetings where grand ideas are described, everyone feels good and, when we leave, nothing happens. What's missing is measureable commitment to change, something against which we can apply resources, track investments, and measure subsequent impact. Marketers are used to testing and measuring. It's the same concept only on a much grander scale.

In our research, the win-win group used the following tools to a much larger degree than the lose-lose group: a multi-period implementation road map, a business case that describes the benefits and investments, and financial commitments from operating budget holders.

The business case *is* the agreement, not a spreadsheet or slide presentation. The business case or funding case is the promise of a benefit based on the availability of resources. It's meaningful only when the executives who have to deliver on the benefit take ownership of the commitment. Nobody else can make that commitment. Simply assigning a target value in a spreadsheet does not create a commitment on the part of the budget holder to deliver.

Our research and experience tell us that committing to the business outcomes is a significant predictor of success. Undoubtedly, this helped eliminate distractions for the executives and is an indicator of their concurrence with the strategy. Leaders need to work with budget holders to help attach value to the changes described in the customer vision and operating approach. Ideally, these change and value discussions should happen concurrently so that budget holder input can help sharpen the vision and prioritize the rollout. You need to agree on the metrics, find the baseline, and get comfortable with the impact either through benchmarks or business analysis. If the stakes are high enough, this could be combined with an operating pilot.

The business case should be allocated to individual projects wherever possible to enable effective tracking of the business impact through a value realization plan. This is a formal way of managing benefits realization so that you can confirm benefits as they occur and monitor real outcomes. If some parts of the effort are not producing the desired results, you want to be in a position to understand what's happening so that you can take corrective actions. This could involve adjustments to the plan or other management interventions in the business-as-usual environment.

Find the right cadence of change. If you want to move slowly and cautiously, reflect that in your plan. This stage is largely about making commitments to the pace of change and the pace of investment. These have to match with the organization's ability to handle change and risk. Build a plan that considers your investment capital and true appetite for change. It should be crystal clear at what points the organization will be under strain, precisely when business benefits can be harvested, and when key expenditures will happen. Keep in mind the biggest investments in money and time are typically up front when foundational changes are being made.

Consider what is already under way, consolidate, and rationalize accordingly. You will probably find that there are already several related projects in your organization that could be assimilated into the bigger change plan. Don't obsess over what might happen in a project plan a year from now; this is a distraction. Our experience shows that overdelivering on a plan in out years impedes success. Instead, keep the big picture with major timelines right and handle detailed planning within the period. Last, the change and milestone planning should be set to maintain enthusiasm and energy toward the project.

One technology company was just finishing what seemed to be a successful come-to-terms meeting. Everybody was nodding along with the change, the team had gone as far as to sign a giant poster as a contract, and they even seemed pleased with the results of this important milestone. The CEO, though, had one last surprise. He announced that he would hire a film documentarian to come in and film at key stages to chronicle the change.

The room fell silent as the group of executives seemed to shrink with fear. One executive finally broke the silence and asked: "You mean we are really going to do this?" It was only with this realization that the real discussions could finally commence.

KEY 5: IMPLEMENTATION AND CHANGE MANAGEMENT— UNAPOLOGETIC EXECUTION

With all preparation and planning complete, it is now time to actually make the changes. The goal is business success here, which, unfortunately, some mistake for milestone success. Hitting milestones is great, but your objective is to create business value, not just complete tasks. The other key goal is to make the change within the original scope, on budget, and on time. This will require making trade-offs and handling issues along the way. Our advice is simple: Be unapologetic about dealing with challenges, including individual people, diverging priorities, or conflicting schedules to name a few. It's the results that matter in execution.

In our research, the win-win group performed the following activities to a much larger degree than the lose-lose group: setting milestones and regularly updating progress reports, creating an internal communication plan to keep affected stakeholders abreast of progress, and launching an operational pilot.

Don't debate strategy during execution. If a condition or underlying assumption has truly changed, then bring it back to the team that built the vision and the plan. Likely, they will reinforce that the vision is still valid and remove the problem rather than alter the approach. Otherwise, once the decision has been made, it's time to march onward.

Good execution is a focused discipline that ensures transparency (good and bad), mitigates obstacles/risk, and avoids distraction. It takes you through the project milestones that collectively produce business outcomes. It's not a time for somebody who didn't win the day during planning to try to again assert his or her preferred strategy now. However, things will come up, so it is perfectly legitimate to finesse the execution plan, letting up a bit if it is too harried and speeding things up that are taking too long.

Keep all eyes on the prize. You'll want a regular communication to the organization that shows progress in order to sustain interest and focus. Early on, celebrating quick wins helps people see progress while also producing benefits that help fund the initiatives. In addition, your organization will likely have transitional periods where the old way isn't quite gone and the new way isn't quite here. These can be frustrating for your teams because they may have to do extra work. If they lose sight of the outcome and focus on the current transitional state, dissent could arise in the form of "This isn't what you promised." Reminding people of the end state and the timeline will help put current inconveniences into perspective.

The communication will take different forms for executives and affected stakeholders. Ultimately, it's about continued engagement. Surprisingly, this is one area that is mostly quickly cut from the plan to save investment resources. Our research and experience showed us that this is a mistake. The win-win segment did this to a large degree, in excess of 2.5 times more than the lose-lose segment, which struggled to get to average half of the time. Clearly, the successful leaders see the value.

Make it a job, not just a role. If this sounds like a lot of work, then you have probably been reading carefully and got the point. It may be tempting to ask one of your executives or managers to play a key role in driving the change execution in addition to performing his or her day job. This halfway tactic is a recipe for problems, as managing complex change requires monitoring and adjusting an array of complex, interrelated work streams. It's better to make it a formal job, staffed with qualified people who are given the necessary resources and authority.

When leaders don't have the time or support to do this properly, they are forced into problem resolution mode, fighting the fires closest to their feet (whether in their day job or in change mode). They can handle breakdowns only after they have happened, rather than being able to stem them off proactively. In addition, when viewed as a side project, change initiatives place leaders in an uncomfortable position, requiring that peers or even higher-ranking executives comply with a plan that may conflict with their day jobs and priorities.

The moral of the story is that if you've followed everything the win-winners do you should be all set. Was it easy? Not likely. Get some help. Everybody needs it.

What's next? Get a reality check.

Determine how prepared your organization is to change. If your initial gut check yields less-than-perfect results, consider it good reason to launch a larger, more formal inquiry into your organization's ability to lead and change.

For a quick assessment of your own position on the CRM change continuum, take a few minutes to answer the following questions:

1. *Is CRM a strategic way of life, or is it a tactical, useful tool?*
   For high-growth and near-ideal organizations, it is a strategic way of life.

2. *What do you think of your insight and your talent?*
   High-growth organizations were more satisfied with their analytics program and the level of their CRM talent. If you had to rate yours based on your gut-check level of satisfaction, what would it be?

3. *How's your leadership style working for you?*
   Or more specifically, when you look at your largest challenges to CRM change, are they characterized by lack of leadership, like the lower-growth organizations surveyed (lack of ownership, mixed priorities, executive sponsorship, etc.)? Or are you dealing with the tactical issues of high-growth organizations, such as data integration?

4. *Do you have win-winners or lose-losers in your CRM organizations?*

   As best you can, think about the correlation between the success of CRM initiatives and the relative success of the careers of the people who are driving them. Is your organization beating the executive's dilemma by fostering win-win environments?

5. *Do you follow the keys to success? And if so, do you do it as much as the win-winners do?*

   In our survey, the win-win group embraced CRM change activities more than the lose-lose group. Review the list and honestly rate your own organization's willingness and success in embracing the five keys presented.

As media and channels continue to proliferate, technology continues to advance, and data continue to explode, CRM will become only more relevant, more complex, and more important to business strategy. It also continually changes, and organizations that want to succeed with their customers must not only change but do it with well-orchestrated precision. This is leadership: the ability to take an organization on a journey to somewhere new, when that somewhere new is always changing. Unfortunately, that means there is never an end to leadership, a time when you can sit back and just manage the status quo. Leadership is change. Become a leader today by getting good at what good leaders do. Is there any other way?

Notes

CHAPTER 1: HISTORY

1. Warren, Chad, "Digital Distress: What Keeps Marketers Up at Night?" *Digital Marketing Blog* (blog), Adobe Systems Incorporated, September 2012, http://blogs.adobe.com/digitalmarketing/digital-marketing/digital-distress-study-what-keeps-marketers-up-at-night/.
2. Olenski, Steve, "Are Brands Wielding More Influence in Social Media Than We Thought?" *Marketshare* (blog), Forbes CMO Network, May 7, 2012. http://www.forbes.com/sites/marketshare/2012/05/07/are-brands-wielding-more-influence-in-social-media-than-we-thought/.

CHAPTER 3: INDUSTRY PERSPECTIVE

1. Moorman, Christine, "The Lure of Disintermediation," *The CMO Survey Blog* (blog), The CMO Survey, December 6, 2010. http://www.cmosurvey.org/blog/the-lure-of-disintermediation/.

2. Strothkamp, Brad, "The Digital Sales Inflection Point: Online Sales Surpass Branch in the U.S.," *Forrester Blogs* (blog), Forrester Research, Inc., May 24, 2012, http://blogs.forrester.com/brad_strot hkamp/12–05–24-the_digital_sales_inflection_point_online_sales_ surpass_branch_in_the_us.

3. ZS Associates, "Oncology Remains Most Restrictive Specialty for Second Year," Press Release, July 30, 2010. http://www.zsassociates.com/about/ news-and-events/oncology-remains-most-restrictive-specialty-for-second-year.aspx.

4. Mangano, John, "Pixels, Patients and Prevention: How Today's Consumers Are Using the Internet to Manage their Health," Speech at the National Conference on Health Communication, Marketing and Media, ComScore, August 2012, http://www.comscore.com/Insights/ Presentations_and_Whitepapers/2012/Online_Health_Trends_2012.

5. Accenture, "Life in the New Normal—The Customer Engagement Revolution," May 2013, http://www.accenture.com/Site CollectionDocuments/PDF/Accenture-Life-in-the-Normal-The-Customer-Engagement-Revolution.pdf.

6. Hensler, Christine, "Generation X Goes Global: Mapping a Youth Culture in Motion," Essay Collection, Routledge, August 2012, http:// www.generationxgoesglobal.com/.

7. Blum, Debra, and Holly Hall, "Donations Barely Rose Last Year as Individuals Held Back," *Chronicle of Philanthropy*, June 17, 2013, http://philanthropy.texterity.com/philanthropy/20130620#pg1.

CHAPTER 5: CUSTOMER STRATEGY

1. Gupta, Sunil, Donald R. Lehmann, and Jennifer Ames Stuart, "Valuing Customers," *Journal of Marketing Research 41*, no. 1 (2004): 7–18, http://papers.ssrn.com/sol3/papers.cfm?abstract_id=459595##.

2. Gupta, Sunil, Dominique Hanssens, Bruce Hardie, Wiliam Kahn, V. Kumar, Nathaniel Lin, Nalini Ravishanker, and S. Sriram, "Modeling Customer Lifetime Value," *Journal of Service Research 9*, no. 2 (November 2006): 139–155, http://www.anderson.ucla.edu/faculty/ dominique.hanssens/content/JSR2006.pdf.

3. van Westendorp, PH, "NSS Price Sensitivity Meter—A New Approach to the Study of Consumer Perception of Price," Proceedings of the 29th Congress, Venice ESOMAR, 1976.

CHAPTER 9: ORGANIZATION AND LEADERSHIP

1. LaValle, Steve, Michael S. Hopkins, Eric Lesser, Rebecca Shockley, and Nina Kruschwitz, "Analytics: The New Path to Value," *MIT Sloan Management Review* (October 24, 2010), http://sloanreview .mit.edu/reports/analytics-the-new-path-to-value/.
2. LaValle, Steve, "Breaking Away with Business Analytics and Optimization," Executive Report, IBM Global Business Services, 2009, http:// www-935.ibm.com/services/uk/gbs/pdf/Breaking_away_with_business_ analytics_and_optimisation.pdf.
3. LaValle et al., 2010.
4. Hagen, Paul, "How Chief Customer Officers Orchestrate Experience," Research Report, Forrester Research, Inc., February 25, 2013, http:// www.forrester.com/How+Chief+Customer+Officers+Orchestrate+ Experiences/fulltext/-/E-RES91181.
5. Hagen, Paul, and Derek Miers, with Harley Manning and Molly Murphy, "Adapt Business Process Improvement for Customer Experience," Research Report, Forrester Research, Inc. January 10, 2013, http:// www.forrester.com/Adapt+Business+Process+Improvement+For+ Customer+Experience/fulltext/-/E-RES87421 and http://www.forrester .com/How+Chief+Customer+Officers+Orchestrate+Experiences/full text/-/E-RES91181.
6. Brosnan, Robert, "Take a Startup Approach to Develop Customer Relationships," Research Report, Forrester Research, Inc., March 19, 2013, http://www.forrester.com/Take+A+Startup+Approach+To+ Develop+Customer+Relationships/fulltext/-/E-RES60912?isTurn Highlighting=true&highlightTerm=marketing%20technology% 20office.
7. Ibid.
8. Hagen and Miers, 2013.

CHAPTER 10: MAKING IT HAPPEN

1. Merkle Case Study: DirecTV. 2009. Advertising Age Custom Programs Showcase. http://brandedcontent.adage.com/merkle2009/ article.php?id=93.

About the Author

David S. Williams is chairman and chief executive officer of Merkle. He acquired Merkle in 1988 and became its twenty-fourth employee. Today, Merkle has more than 2,000 employees in locations in the United States, China, and the United Kingdom.

Under David's leadership, Merkle has sustained greater than 20 percent annual growth over the past 25 years and was recognized as a market leader by Forrester Research. In 2013, *Advertising Age* ranked Merkle as the twenty-second largest agency of any discipline worldwide and the seventh largest customer relationship marketing (CRM)/direct agency in the United States. In 2012, Merkle was named to the "Ten Agencies to Watch" list in *Advertising Age*'s A-List Issue. David was recognized by Winning Workplaces and *Fortune* magazine as one of America's Best Bosses of 2006 and was the 2007 Maryland Ernst & Young Entrepreneur of the Year.

David served for six years (2006–2011) on the board of directors of the Direct Marketing Association, where he also served on its Executive Committee. He served for three years (2010–2013) as a member of the board of trustees at the Howard County General Hospital, a member of Johns Hopkins Medicine. David is a frequent speaker at industry events and has written numerous articles and white papers about topics such as customer relationship marketing, database marketing and analytics, digital media, and marketing technology.

He began his career at Butcher & Singer, a Philadelphia-based investment bank, and holds a bachelor of science in business administration from Shippensburg University in Pennsylvania.

David can be reached at davidwilliams@connectedcrm.com.

About Merkle

Merkle is a market leader in technology-enabled, data-driven customer relationship marketing (CRM). For more than 25 years, Fortune 1000 companies and leading nonprofit organizations have partnered with Merkle to drive revenue and profit growth through relevant, personal, and timely customer interactions. Serving GEICO, DirecTV, Dell, MetLife, Lowe's, AARP, and other market-leading brands, Merkle is purpose-built to leverage a full range of consulting, technology, analytical, and digital agency services to create programs that place the customer at the center of the business strategy.

Merkle delivers its solutions and capabilities through a Connected CRM approach, which provides a systematic framework for identifying, serving, and retaining customers based on their value, through orchestrated interactions that improve financial results, create competitive advantage, and drive shareholder value.

The company has experienced a compound annual growth rate of more than 20 percent over the past 25 years, with 2013 revenues topping $350 million. With more than 2,000 employees, the privately held corporation is headquartered in Columbia, Maryland, with additional offices in Boston, Denver, Hagerstown, Little Rock, London, Minneapolis, Montvale, Nanjing, New York City, Philadelphia, Pittsburgh, San Francisco, and Shanghai.

Connected CRM is a trademark owned by Merkle Inc.

Index